I HAVE A GOOD LIFE

I HAVE

The Story of

A GOOD

Adrian's Healing

LIFE

Marian Nygard

I Have a Good Life
Copyright © 2016 Marian Nygard

Edited by Robert Neely
Cover/Layout: Blake Berg

Published by 3DM Publishing
ISBN 978-0-9965300-8-8

3DM Publishing
3dmpublishing.com

CONTENTS

FOREWORD

I am often asked what is the greatest miracle I've ever witnessed firsthand. It's always a challenging question for many reasons, as miracles are hard to categorize. But having said that, Adrian's healing is certainly in the top five—and maybe the top three, out of thousands.

I was there when the miracle took place. I'll never forget the joy that filled the room the night Adrian stood with his parents and testified of what had just happened. It was an indescribable moment. People stood and cheered, praising God for an extended period of time, for they had just witnessed something that only God Himself could accomplish. He healed a young man from such a tormenting affliction. Adrian's newfound freedom was palpable.

This amazing family made another trip to Bethel a reasonably short time after their initial trip. They testified again, this time of the creative miracles of newly formed muscles, and were also able to give us their doctor's reports confirming the things they told us previously. Once again we stood to give the One who is worthy, praise.

Following their visits to Redding I met them once again in Norway. This time Adrian brought me a gift—a beautiful hunting knife that he picked out and purchased for me. It is one of my most prized possessions. It came from a grateful young man who got his life back.

I mention my privileged exposure to this family for only one reason: I know their story. I've watched it unfold, and have rejoiced with them over the abundance of God's goodness in their lives. But even so, I wept and wept throughout this book. To be honest, that caught me off guard. It's not as though tears are that foreign to me. They're not. They're actually quite common. It's just that I knew what to expect, and it still got me. I'm just glad I didn't read it on a plane, or in an airport club. Instead my tears fell quietly in my living room, making explanations unnecessary.

I was deeply moved over many things: the grief they went through for years before their miracle, and the courage they expressed throughout the ordeal. The challenges they had to face just to survive were beyond comprehension. The impossible challenge of getting Adrian to Bethel, with all the medical equipment that kept him alive, and yet the uncompromising dedication to do whatever God said. I was rocked over their honesty throughout the book. They did not work to project a greater faith than they actually had, nor did they dumb down their confidence in God to appear humble. This book is a masterpiece in honesty—refreshingly so. I was greatly impacted by the honor they gave to the medical community during the whole ordeal. Their story at this point could be considered a manual of "what to do if you think you're in the middle of a miracle." It was that good. The way they navigated the challenge with family and friends is honestly material I've never heard anyone talk about in this measure before. It is filled with such a profound measure of divine wisdom.

I was deeply moved by their comments about the presence of God, and Bethel's value for this greatest of all gifts from God. They gave us honor for our value of Him, and not the miracle, which was perfect!! The miracle was not our doing.

Miracles are gifts from God. As His servants we sometimes get to be involved. But our role, while honorable in nature, is nothing more than what the postman does when he delivers a check in the mail. He didn't write it. And while we're thankful he brought it to us, we know to give thanks to the one who wrote the check. Jesus is to be praised, for He paid the price in full for Adrian's healing—and mine, and yours.

I sincerely want everyone I know to read this story. It is packed with practical faith, and extreme wisdom. Read it and be changed!

Bill Johnson
Bethel Church, Redding, CA
Author of *When Heaven Invades Earth,* and Co-author of *The Essential Guide to Healing*

PREFACE

Dear reader,

This is our story. And at the same time it's not.
We can't take credit for what God has done. It's his story.
It just happened to take place in the life of our family.

For 12 years we experienced about every feeling known to man.
We thought the path of our lives was pretty much settled and
braced ourselves for the tremendous grief that was to come.

Then God intervened. A miracle 12 years in the making.

Within minutes everything changed. We got hope! We were given
a future.

Words cannot begin to express our gratitude, but that will not stop
us from trying.

To our wonderful, healing Papa God: Thank you. We love you. All
we are and have is yours.

My family and I would like to thank Bill, Eric, Heidi, Martin and Irene, Mike and Sally, Marla, Elin, Pam, Knut, Tina and Sissel. You are such a blessing to us. We are honored to be doing life with you.

To my beloved husband and our wonderful children: Thank you. I love you. Always.

I pray that our story will bring life and restoration to you as you read. He will do it again.

God bless you.

Marian Nygard

"I could never have done that to my child," she shrugged and said, all the while focused on something distant.

I didn't get what she meant, so I waited for her to continue. The woman had approached me gently, but clearly with something weighing on her mind.

"Are you Adrian's mother?"

I nodded.

It turned out that her child had been born with a handicap. "I would never have anyone pray for her healing," she said. "That would have been equal to saying that she wasn't good enough. I love her just the way she is."

She shrugged, as if to demonstrate the difference between us. She loved her handicapped child. I had someone pray for mine.

SLEEPLESS NIGHTS AND ENDLESS DAYS

O nly four hours passed from the very first pains of labor until he saw the light of day. Swift yet brutally painful for a first-time mom.

The midwife looked surprised when we asked if the baby was healthy and even more when we asked her to check that there had been no breach of the baby's oxygen supply during the birth. That was probably not the most common question from happy new parents, but we had two nephews both affected by cerebral palsy as a result of complications during birth or illness shortly after birth. We wanted to be certain. So our son was examined extensively, and was thankfully declared completely healthy.

Then they put this tiny bloodstained bundle on my stomach. Almost unnoticeably he started moving up and forward, searching for food, millimeter by millimeter. It was the most amazing experience I have ever had.

All hospital personnel left the delivery room, dimming the lights, so we could have some alone time to get to know our little boy. We studied him as he rested on my chest. So unbelievably beautiful! We savored the name that we had chosen for him: Adrian. Yes, the name suited him. He looked like a tiny Adrian. My husband, Thomas, crawled into the hospital bed with me, and we memorized every feature of our little baby.

Then we gave him to God.

We thanked him for allowing us to parent this wonderful, precious little boy. We acknowledged that he was God's, and we gave thanks for letting us borrow him. There, in the dim light of the delivery room, we asked God to strengthen our newborn son, to fill him with his Spirit, and to guide him through life. It was the best birthday gift we could give our son. We gave him back.

We had been married for eight years before becoming fulltime parents. Until then we had served as a weekend foster home for several children. We had noticed that it was easy for us to love children who were not biologically ours.

Before we had any children we traveled a lot, lived and worked abroad, and experienced new cultures. So when Adrian was born, it was not very difficult for us to get settled in another completely new culture—being the parents of small children!

The first months of Adrian's life were busy but uncomplicated. He was a wonderful little baby who responded easily and communicated clearly that he preferred company. So at church and within the family, he naturally shifted from one set of arms to another. He was surrounded by people who loved him, and he loved it. Adrian also loved whenever our bonus kids came over. He adored when they sung for him, played with him, or just cuddled him.

Life was good and easy for those first months.

Then, all of a sudden, it wasn't.

As a baby Adrian was fed breast milk only. However, when he was almost six months, the public health nurse strongly suggested that we should give him baby food. She hoped that more solid foods would help him sleep sounder at night. To the tired new parents, that sounded attractive. Adrian was an absolute night owl who preferred to be fed and cuddled at night, and we were in a serious sleep deficit after several months.

Both Thomas and I have minor allergies to pollen and animals, so we made sure that we stayed clear of possible allergens in any baby food to prevent Adrian from having an allergic reactions. We took every precaution, and soon we were looking forward to finally getting some sleep at night.

We couldn't have been more wrong.

Adrian was bending backward in pain. He screamed until his face reddened and his clothes were soaked with sweat. His pain was especially excruciating at night, and he was inconsolable. We took turns carrying him through the night. It was awful.

This kind of hysterical crying gets to you. As a parent, you become so distressed by these constant screams of agony that you become in danger of acting irrationally. My husband and I each could only stand to be alone with him for a maximum of 30 minutes. Then we had to switch. We bent his knees toward his stomach and paced back and forth in our bedroom, cradling him in our arms. That was the only time he got any relief from the intense pain, but even then he kept on screaming and crying inconsolably.

I was so tired I could no longer think. Every time it was Thomas' turn to carry our baby, I fell almost unconscious on the bed, entering into a coma as soon as my head hit the pillow. I didn't even notice that Adrian continued screaming hysterically next to me.

All I knew was that if I intended to get any sleep that night, that was my window of opportunity. Then I got up half an hour later to switch with Thomas, and it was his turn to tip unconsciously into bed.

The only times Adrian calmed down slightly were when he was nursing. Even then he sobbed quietly. It was heartbreaking not to be able to console our child.

The public health nurse and the pediatrician claimed that it was normal for babies to experience discomfort while transitioning from breast milk to more solid foods and that this would naturally improve with time. In hindsight, we have concluded that they couldn't possibly have understood how ill Adrian actually was. We have realized that a lot of parents come to the medical clinic and complain about crying and lack of sleep, and that statements such as "I am up all night because he is screaming" often translate to the parents being up a couple of times during the night, giving the baby the pacifier, and going back to sleep. That was not our situation. We were up all night with a baby screaming at the top of his lungs, unable to respond to any contact due to horrendous pain. That was what we explained to the doctors. That was probably not what they heard. They told us that having a baby was equally hard on every new parent and that we just needed to hang in there.

We reached a breakthrough when Adrian was seven months old. During coffee at church, the unmistakable odor of a well-filled diaper lingered in the room, and I laughed: "Yes, that would be my son! Sorry, guys, I'll change his diaper." One of the other mothers looked surprised and said that it was her boy who needed his diapers changed. She said that the reason his diapers smelled so badly was because gluten had passed through his system without being digested. I was taken aback. Surely, we had not given Adrian any gluten! Could it be that something else was passing through his digestive system without being processed?

We contacted our family physician, and he contacted our local hospital. We were put on a waiting list. Now that we had realized something was wrong with our baby, we made numerous calls to speed up the process. Nevertheless we had to wait for three months before they agreed to see him at the hospital. By then we had had an inconsolable, screaming baby for five months. Again, I don't think any of the professionals realized how very sick he was.

The first doctor who examined him at the hospital for sure

didn't realize anything. She appeared to have a preconceived opinion of the diagnosis being lactose intolerance. If mom laid off the dairy products, that would solve the problem, the doctor claimed. We were asked to come back for another appointment in six weeks. But when we got the record by mail afterward, we read how the doctor had stated several symptoms that Adrian supposedly had displayed. None of them were real. The symptoms we actually had described at the doctor's office were never included.

That was our first encounter with the local hospital, and we were understandably disillusioned. I dutifully obeyed the doctor's orders and followed a strict non-dairy diet, but the baby kept on screaming. The nights were the worst; he was inconsolable. We were completely exhausted. In the midst of all this, Thomas continued to go to work as usual. I don't understand how we managed, but then again, what were our options? You simply do what you have to.

I was on this non-dairy diet until Adrian was eleven and a half months old. Following the advice from the hospital, I reduced nursing, and Adrian starting eating normal, home-cooked baby food. That turned out to be a disastrous decision.

He had started toddling and eventually walking when he was ten months old. Now all of a sudden he stopped. Whenever he tried to stand up, he tipped over and fell. He clung to the wall to remain standing. Soon he went back to crawling.

This change made Adrian's medical team come to life. Neurologists who had different theories as to why he could no longer walk examined Adrian. He became more withdrawn and switched between being completely passive and absolutely hyperactive. Sometimes he banged his head against the wall or the floor.

Adrian had turned into a shadow of himself. Apparently our happy little son was gone, but we knew that he was still in there somewhere. We got small glimpses of him now and then. It made us realize how much pain he was in most of the time. Whenever he was angry or despairing, he took whatever was at hand and threw it at Thomas and me. We felt relieved when he did this, because at least we knew that he was still able to express the frustration he was feeling.

I tried to describe how ill he was to the doctors at the hospital but ended up feeling that I was the one banging my head against the wall. I later realized that parents often exaggerate the symptoms of their children or quote the symptoms they have found on the Internet rather than describing the actual problems of their child. It must be difficult for doctors to separate fiction from reality. But in my experience, the result of all this is a slightly passive, noncommittal attitude at the early stages of the examination of very ill children. The fact that doctors didn't act on my description of how ill Adrian actually was came as a complete shock to me.

I remember an appointment at the hospital when all the attending physicians circled around Adrian, who was sitting on the floor playing with a toy. One of doctors looked inquiringly at me before asking: "Would you describe him as being hyperactive now?"

I had to force myself not to laugh hysterically! That was not the right question to ask a mother who had not slept for a year! I felt like answering yes just to get some reaction and see if these doctors were still alive. Instead I answered politely: "No, he is not hyperactive now. As you can see, he is sitting calmly on the floor playing. When he is hyperactive, he is spinning around without any goal or purpose. That's when he throws things and aims at us, his parents. Like the other day when he was angry with me for not allowing him to play with the toilet seat, and he responded by taking the wooden toilet roll stand and swinging it straight at my head, resulting in me passing out on the bathroom floor. That was an example of when he was slightly hyperactive."

The doctor studied me before she looked at the boy playing quietly on the floor. Then she scribbled something in her notepad. I was left feeling that she was wondering which of the two of us she should admit.

The hospital instructed us to put Adrian on a wide range of diets. First one specific type of carbs, then another. Deanimated amino acids, with analgesics to see if his body could accept any nutrients. Everything had to be tested so any possible cause had to be eliminated. He threw up many times daily, and each diaper was completely liquid. Meanwhile, he continued having painful days and nights so excruciating that words fail to describe them.

He didn't walk any longer—he just crawled. If I put him down on the floor next to the box of books, he sat and looked at the books without showing any interest in exploring the room or playing with anything else. If I took him over to the window, he studied the birds outside without even noticing that he had thrown up and that the contents of his stomach were now running down the glass of the window. He got used to constantly being sick.

We got used to it too. Of course, we kept hoping that Adrian would get better, but we had come to understand that the examinations at the hospital would be a long, time-consuming process. So when Thomas got an offer to visit a church in Chicago, we thought it would be a good idea. We didn't give much thought to the fact that he got the tickets really, really cheap as it was right after 9/11. It was only an eight-day trip. What could possibly happen in eight days?

Thomas had not been away for more than a couple of days before Adrian was admitted to hospital. He didn't put on any weight. His head was normal size, but compared to the tiny, frail little body, it looked gigantic. I could no longer get his sweet little head through the neck of the minuscule onesies that actually fit his body.

Finally, Adrian had been assigned a doctor who managed to see him as he really was. He admitted him as an emergency and instructed that he should be fed intravenously. I was looking forward to Adrian actually keeping some nutrition. My friends talked about how their babies kept on outgrowing their baby clothes before even getting to wear them. Adrian was now 13 1/2 months old but was still wearing size 6-9 months. All his clothes were completely worn out because I refused to buy any new ones, as I was waiting for him to grow. He was the only baby I knew of who had worn out his jeans to the point that they actually had holes in the knees.

I dreaded the idea of having to call Thomas to tell him what had happened. I even considered not doing it because I desperately wanted him to be able to relax on his trip to the U.S. More than anything, I wanted him to be able to sleep peacefully at night. After a year of hardly any sleep, that was what he needed the most. But we had agreed that I was to call him if anything happened, and he had left only because I had promised to do so. I considered how I would have reacted if my husband had failed to inform me that our son were admitted to a hospital. I knew that if he failed to tell me, I would have nailed him to a wall—if not physically, then most certainly verbally. There was no other way; I had to call him.

He was completely heartbroken and felt horrible about not being able to be there while Adrian was in the hospital. We agreed that he would stay in Chicago until the scheduled date for his return and that I would call him if the situation got any worse.

This was the first of countless hospital admissions for Adrian. In hindsight, we have often pondered how fortunate we were not to know anything about what was in store for us. We were waiting for the doctors to find out what Adrian was allergic to in order for us to keep him away from whatever made him sick. Surely it couldn't be any worse than that.

Thomas came home and was shocked to see how little and frail Adrian was. I had not noticed. When you see someone every day, these subtle changes in appearance tend to pass unnoticed. However, I had started to cut open the neckband of every onesie to get his head through.

We noticed that Adrian cried less when he was on intravenous nutrition. The nurses smiled and said that the children were often more compliant once they found themselves assimilated into the comforting rhythm of the hospital routine, but that was not the case for Adrian. The boy that we knew to be hidden in there somewhere peaked out whenever the pain disappeared. He smiled more, was more talkative, and had the energy to play. He proudly grinned as one parent pushed the child's tractor through the hospital corridors, while the other ran like crazy, trying to keep up while clutching the IV stand. He could stand up and walk a little, and he seemed to be gaining strength.

The doctors decided that since the intestines had been given some rest, we should try feeding him enteral nutrition products from a baby bottle. Within a short period of time, he stopped walking, he no longer had the strength to play, he screamed out in pain, and he banged his head in the bedside or on the floor. He was pale and exhausted.

I still remember the moment when the fourth neurologist who examined him concluded: "I know why he keeps on falling whenever he tries to walk. He is in so much pain that he can't stand up. He bangs his head to divert his attention from the excruciating pain in his stomach."

Something burst within me. This was exactly what we had been feeling without being able to prove it. I felt so extremely sorry for my son. How could such a tiny, little boy be in such tremendous pain!

Adrian went through surgery to get a temporary intravenous line to spare the thin veins of his arms. For a period of time he was given all nutrition intravenously, and once again he blossomed. He didn't sleep well at night. As he was given the energy mainly during the night, his sleep was light and easily interrupted, and often he laid awake for hours in the middle of the night. We were OK with that, as long as he wasn't in pain.

The hospital staff told us that Adrian might need the IV nutrition for weeks or months. We rejoiced every day as he was able to play. He smiled and laughed, and we recognized the baby that we had had known for a few months before everything had changed.

Thomas struggled to incorporate into our new life after the trip to Chicago. He had to be present for Adrian, but also for me, because I was exhausted after having done both day and night shifts at the hospital. Now and then we got to talk quietly for a few minutes while Adrian was sleeping, and I asked him about the trip. He said it was OK, but that he had felt misplaced and longed to be with us at the hospital. I felt sorry that he hadn't benefitted more from the long journey and from the sacrifice that he had made.

"But I got something," he said. There was intensity to his voice and a sparkle in his eye that had not been present before he left. "There was one preacher. I didn't get his name, and I can hardly remember anything of what he said. I was unable to focus because I could only think of you two. But he told us this story of a tradition that his family had. Each year they placed an ornament on the Christmas tree that would represent something from the year gone by that they were truly grateful for. That touched me!"

It touched me, too. From time to time you run into revelations, small or great, that you know will change your life. This was one of those occasions. There, in the darkness, while Adrian slept in the hospital bed next to us, we made a decision always to honor whatever we had to be grateful for. We decided that we would celebrate it at Christmas every year and make sure to give God the glory for everything that he continuously does in our lives.

The temporary IV line was replaced by a permanent one. Adrian's homecoming was closing in, and the hospital arranged for us to go through an intensive training period in specialized medical care. The thin, white tube that surfaced from Adrian's chest was to be treated with sterile medical procedures only. Late at night in the hospital, two tired parents made use of the few hours of Adrian's sleep to practice putting on sterile gloves without touching the outside, connecting IV sets and tubes without contaminating the connections, filling syringes, preparing sterile areas, and connecting our child to sterile infusions through his IV line without infecting him.

All of these procedures can be taught. It may have been exhausting and at times difficult, but all of this knowledge can be acquired. How to parent your child while complying with this regime of medical procedures was a much more complex lesson.

Our little 15-month-old child was wide-eyed as he paid attention to Mommy and Daddy going through the sterile procedures and preparing to connect him to his IV nutrition. Hidden behind the surgical mask, Daddy chatted with him and explained everything that we were going to do. The nurses in charge of teaching us came to hold Adrian firmly so he wouldn't get near the sterile connections. We refused because we didn't want anybody to hold Adrian against his will. That was not how we wanted to parent, and our responsibility as parents was more important to us than anything else. Adrian paid full attention as we told him that he had to lie completely still. Then I sang a Norwegian children's song as I disinfected his catheter and prepared to connect him to the IV line. I sang through all the procedures, and Adrian lay still, following my every move with his eyes. The second I stopped singing he was up and about, playing with his toys. We realized that we had found a key—it was possible to execute complex medical procedures without sacrificing being nurturing and protective parents.

We couldn't protect Adrian from all harm. He had to go through countless exams and surgeries, and at times we felt powerless. Several times I had to fight the urge to grab my kid and just run. Instead I had to stay strong, safe, and predictable. It was our responsibility as parents to remain solid as rocks—rocks he could cling to and rocks that could carry the weight of everything that his life would imply. Our job was to comfort, receive, embrace, and contain.

We returned home to a new life. From now on, we did sterile procedures morning and evening. Adrian was connected to the intravenous nutrition throughout the night. He needed attention 24/7. Daddy applied for financial aid from social services, because taking care of Adrian was a full-time job for both of us.

After a while we received help from the local authorities, and a nurse came to watch Adrian two nights a week while we slept. The other nights we watched over him ourselves. This strange life somehow became a routine. It is weird how you can get used to extreme conditions if you have to. We could see that Adrian was comfortable, so everything else ceased to matter. The fact that we spent most of the 24 hours of each day caring and attending to him was not important. Running up and down the stairs carrying heavy IV stands became a daily routine. We set IV pumps and handled medical equipment as if we had done it all our lives. We drew blood samples at home, filled out blood requisition forms, and delivered them to the hospital. It became important to us to do as much as possible at home so that Adrian wouldn't have to spend so much time in the hospital. Our wonderful doctor made sure that we were able to do so.

Adrian flourished. He talked and laughed, and it was a joy to see that he finally was well. We felt like a normal family. The fact that no other families lived like us didn't matter. Our son was feeling fine, and nothing else mattered.

Obviously, there were bumps along the way. After a few months on IV nutrition, Adrian had to go through another round of testing ordinary nutrients through his digestive tract. The doctors were fully determined not to let Adrian remain on IV nutrition if there was any hope whatsoever of his body ever accepting an ordinary diet, and so they kept on testing him repeatedly. Adrian had a MicKey—a little button connected to a gastric tube, fit surgically into his stomach to see if he could possibly handle minuscule amounts such as 20 ml/hour passing through his intestines. No luck. We tried everything, but it was as if we were feeding him pesticides. He became terribly ill.

The doctors finally concluded that this little boy could not digest food and didn't have any nutritional absorption in his intestines, confirming what we had suspected for some time without being able to prove it. We prepared for a life that most likely would be quite different from most people's lives.

CONSTANTLY INCONSTANT

It's strange what you can get used to. Adrian was pain free, and so life was brilliant. The fact that he had to go through sterile medical procedures morning and night; that he had to be connected to his IV line for 14 hours every night; that he had to receive medical care 24/7— none of that mattered. Adrian didn't have any pain, and life was easy. We couldn't have asked for more.

After a while, the nurses started coming several nights a week to watch over Adrian, and we got some much-needed sleep. We still were woken up whenever Adrian was in pain so we could administer all the IV medication and nutrition ourselves. Thomas could no longer continue in his job, so he received a certain financial aid from social services, which allowed him to take care of the medical needs of his son. Somehow life once again stabilized, and we felt we were on the right track.

At the same time as these events, we were asked to become a foster home for our bonus kids. They had been visitng our home frequently for many years and were an integrated part of our family. We accepted, and Adrian was thrilled to have his siblings with him permanently. That year a new ornament adorned the Christmas tree: birds finding their way to the nest. Our family had been blessed with more members, and we were grateful.

An aside: As a foster family, we are subject to the Norwegian law of Children's Services, which means we are bound by confidentiality. Therefore, I won't discuss our foster children in this book. If it were up to us, we would like to shout out from every mountaintop exactly how much we love them and just how much they mean to us. But for now, we will have to settle with saying that each and every one of them has his or her own wonderful story and that all of them have so much to give the world.

The very same morning that our bonus kids moved in for good, Adrian, now two years old, was admitted to the hospital with a high fever. We surmised it was it some kind of infection, so Thomas took Adrian to the hospital while I was at home with our other children. The doctors did not find evidence of any infection, so we didn't give it much thought. After all, Adrian would soon get better, right? Young children spike a fever all the time. We had contacted the hospital as a precaution because he had an IV line, not because we were particularly worried. Little did we know that that was the first of many, many emergency admissions.

Adrian went from playing cheerfully with a normal body temperature in one second, to shaking uncontrollably with a fever of 105.8 °F fifteen minutes later. We stopped counting the times we had to speed to the waiting doctors at the children's ward of the hospital. Before long, hardly fifteen minutes passed from the second we observed the first symptom until we arrived at the hospital, because we knew the routine. Despite our haste, we were reproached several times by the hospital staff for having waited too long before taking him to the hospital. Adrian got seriously ill within a very short time frame, so we got used to always being on alert.

As a result, we got really good at living in the present. If Adrian was "healthy," with no fever, life was good. We enjoyed ourselves and celebrated all the ordinary days. Whenever Adrian was sick and in the hospital, it was important to us not to blow things out of proportion. Our excellent doctor at the local hospital made sure we had information, knowledge and perspective, and he contributed to our sense of safety. As Adrian stabilized after each emergency episode, we took him home as soon as we possibly could and continued the intravenous medication regime ourselves at home. Specialized medical care became a part of our daily routine; so much so that none of our kids found it strange to see Mom and Dad mixing IV medication or connecting their little brother to IV fluids. It meant a lot to us to be allowed to remain a "normal" family—at least as normal as we could be.

It turned out that Adrian had an immune deficiency that made him extremely ill every time he got sick. His blood values were alarming. For a period of time, Adrian was admitted to the hospital every fifteen days with emergency episodes. Only twice did he have bacterial growth in his blood samples—once after having been connected to the IV medication by a nurse, and the other time after surgery. All the other times he was admitted with acute illness, no underlying infection that could explain his symptoms was discovered, leaving it impossible to prevent anything similar from happening again.

Once the catheter made a small tear in his heart, and within a short period of time, the atrium filled with a substance that was considered to be fungus. Adrian was flown to another hospital, and we remained in a cardio and cancer ward for two months while he was being treated. Thomas was at home with our children, and I cared for Adrian around the clock at the hospital. He was so ill! At one point, my brother and a friend came to visit. Later they told me that they had been sure they would never see Adrian again because they couldn't possibly imagine that he would survive.

On several occasions we felt unsure whether we would get to take Adrian home from the hospital. The doctors spoke of these emergency episodes as "potentially life-threatening situations." Adrian noticed the decay within his own body. When we were hospitalized at the cancer and cardio ward, he experienced death firsthand when several of the children that he knew passed away.

He knew that not only old people died, but that children could become so ill that they could no longer live.

When Thomas and I were both at the hospital, one of us could take Adrian out of the room while the other parent talked to the doctor. It was important for us to shield him as much as possible, because we didn't want him to be a part of "grown-up" conversations. When I was alone with Adrian at the hospital, I depended on the nurses to take care of him during the conversations with the doctors. They usually had time to do so, but not always. That became painfully apparent to me one day when I was playing with Adrian, and he suddenly said: "You're sick, mommy, and I'm a doctor. Now I have to take a stick and poke it in your heart, 'cause you have a lump in there. It's going to hurt really, really badly, and you will cry, but I just have to do it."

My heart broke as I realized that my little boy of 2-1/2 years had listened in while the doctors had explained how they were considering taking a biopsy from the mass in his heart. His words kept on ringing in my ears for the rest of the day: It's going to hurt really badly, but I just have to do it!

No matter how much we wanted to protect him from all pain, sometimes we couldn't. In those moments, our task was to be there with him through all pain. Sometimes it just slipped out: "I wish I could do this for you, Adrian! I wish that I was sick instead!"

When I said something like that, he stared at me with a terrified look on his face and violently shook his head: "Oh no, Mommy! I don't want you to be in pain!"

One time, we visited the kindergarten, when parents were invited to an art exhibition. The images the kids had created were neatly framed and hanging on the wall. They also sold cakes and coffee at the event to raise money for charity.

Adrian met us in the hallway. He was thrilled that we had come to the exhibition, and he guided us to the paintings that he had done. They were beautiful. We were happy to pay for them, and the artwork was marked as sold with a tiny red sticker. We had to wait until the next day to collect the masterpieces; after all, we didn't want to ruin the exhibition.

We found a vacant spot and sat down. Adrian was happy and chatted eagerly about everything they had made and all the preparations they had done for the great exhibition.

"We have to get a lot of money" he grinned.

I knew that the charity that they were raising funds for was an organization helping handicapped children in other countries, but I was unsure whether Adrian knew that . I decided to ask him.

He answered promptly.

"The money goes to glutton and feather!" he beamed.

I hesitated. I sensed that my three-year-old knew perfectly well what he wanted to say, but that was not it. He repeated his answer with exaggerated facial expressions and infinite patience with his slow mother.

"The money goes to glutton and feather! You know; gluttons and feathers!"

He looked enquiringly at me to see if I got it. I didn't. My expression remained equally blank and bewildered.

He sighed and pointed at himself.

"The children with glutton and feather! Like me!"

It finally dawned on me. He had certainly understood the purpose of the exhibition! Helping handicapped children; like him—he who had a button and a catheter.

He nodded happily now that his slow mother finally had understood what he was saying.

"So we need to raise a lot of money," he said, "to make sure that they get what they need."

I blinked a tear away while I hurried to pay $15 for a piece of cake. No, no change, please. We had to raise a lot of funds. There was a lot at stake. I was so terrifyingly aware of what Adrian's life might have looked like if he had been born in another country, in other circumstances. What if he had been born somewhere where "glutton and feather" was not an option? Where nobody footed the bill for intravenous nutrition and expensive medication? The thought sent shivers down my spine.

Adrian had understood it. Those who have access to privileges have a special responsibility.

———————————

Thomas waited for me at the top of the stairs. He had been crying.
"Go and talk to Adrian," he said. "He has something to tell you."

Without another word he turned around and returned to our bedroom.

I followed the hallway to Adrian's room. He was lying in his bed with huge headphones on, and he smiled as he spotted me. Ever since he was 15 months old, he had loved listening to audiobooks. Now he turned off his CD player and crawled out of his bed before climbing the sofa to sit on my lap.

"Hi! Daddy says that you have something to tell me."

"Yes!" Adrian beamed toward me. "Jesus said that I had to tell you that he will be coming to get me soon!"

It felt like a blow straight to my face. Our three-year-old was a verbal little kid with a lot on his mind, but not for a second did I think that he was fantasizing or exaggerating. I recognized the authority in what he said, and I knew that what he told me was true.

Adrian was not affected at all and continued his story of how Jesus had taken him to heaven, how he had recognized several of the children there; how he and Jesus had baked a pizza together, and how they had danced and played.

"At first I cried when Jesus said what he would come and get me soon. I thought that the two of you would be really sad." His eyes were wide and serious. "But after I had been with Jesus for a while, he said it was time for me to go back. Then I cried because I couldn't be with him, anymore. But he said that in a short while I could come back."

Adrian jumped cheerfully off the coach and sat down on the floor to play with his toys. I remained seated for a while, observing him playing before shuffling out of his room. He wanted to listen to the rest of his audiobook.

Only when I saw Thomas lying tear-stained on our bed did all the built-up sadness erupt into spastic sobbing. I cried with my head buried in his chest, staying quiet so the children wouldn't get scared. Soul-wrenching wailing burst its way out of my body. None of us said anything.

After a while Thomas got up. "Take your time," he said. He went to the bathroom to splash some cold water on his face. Then he went downstairs to help the kids and make breakfast.

For the next two days, we functioned this way. We took turns grieving. One of us closed the door to our bedroom for half an hour at a time and cried out everything that wouldn't fit into words, while the other took care of the kids and the household. Then we switched.

After two days, we were ready to celebrate his life instead of grieving over the fact that it might be short. I sat down and wrote Adrian's dream and the date: June 7, 2003.

"**G**ranny often says: 'Oh, you poor thing!' to me, Mommy. Why does she do that?"

I smiled. There was no doubt that the three-year-old had interpreted the situation correctly. My mother had always been proud to cook for her great family. The fact that her youngest grandson was unable to relish her cooking was hard for her to cope with. To her it felt like excluding someone.

"It's quite possible that Granny feels sorry for you," I commented.

"Why? It's not like I'm sick or anything!" Adrian said, slightly surprised.

When he said this, we were heading toward kindergarten for the two hours he could actually stand being there, as long as he slept for one of them. It was funny to see how he didn't define himself as being sick. On other occasions, he grinned and said, "I'm sicker than all of these people combined!" It was actually possible for him to harbor two thoughts at the same time.

I considered carefully before answering Adrian's question about his grandmother. It was important not to raise Adrian as a victim. We didn't want him to walk around feeling sorry for himself. Equally, we wanted him to be realistic about his own disease and condition. We had experienced that he was left with a higher sense of accomplishment when he balanced these apparent contradictions.

"The fact that you can't eat is difficult for Granny. That's probably why she feels sorry for you."

He pondered it before nodding thoughtfully:

"Yes, that might be the case. Food is really important to Granny."

It was hard for him when he first started on intravenous nutrition. He was used to eating and missed having something in his mouth. It was heartbreaking to see my one-and-a-half-year-old boy lying on the kitchen floor trying to dismantle the grate under the fridge because he had a glimpse of a breadcrumb behind the refrigerator grill. Or maybe it was a dust bunny? It didn't matter, because it would have ended up in his mouth either way. He was totally absorbed as he struggled to dismantle the grate and was completely furious at me for trying to distract him. Brushing his teeth became the highlight of the day because he finally had something tasty in his mouth.

For the first six months Adrian was on intravenous nutrition, one of us would take him for a stroll while the rest of the family ate. We didn't want to torment him by making him watch others eat when he couldn't. As the intravenous nutrition gradually increased in volume, Adrian stopped being hungry. He had also realized the connection between having food in his mouth and having excruciating pain in his stomach, and he didn't want to be in pain anymore. As long as he didn't eat, he didn't have any pain in his stomach or intestines. His quality of life increased dramatically, and he was happy. He began to ask to be present at the meals, and he loved cooking with his dad.

Adrian developed an excellent sense of smell. Whenever he passed a meal that left cooking on the stove, he exclaimed, "Mmm! This smells lovely! I can tell there are sundried tomatoes and basil in this!"

But his excellent nose was not always a plus. Several nurses were told to leave his room in the wee hours of the morning after having eaten sandwiches with garlic in them while at work, or having used a heavily fragranced hair conditioner. Failure to remove the smell resulted in Adrian throwing up violently.

He soon learned to take the feeling of others into consideration. Even when he had to tell garlic-smelling nurses to leave his room, he shouted as they were leaving: "I'm really sorry! But either you leave, or I'll puke!"

It certainly was a steep learning curve for the nurses.

Whenever Adrian visited somebody, he often experienced how the hostesses were embarrassed when they discovered that he could not eat. What could they serve him when he couldn't have any of the food they had prepared? Often he said something comforting, assuring them he was fine. He wasn't hungry, and besides, he liked sitting next to the others while they ate. The miserable look on the face of the mothers clearly showed that those words only made it worse. Was he really going to sit there and watch the other children eat? Adrian never made any fuss about it, nor did the other children. The adults struggled more to come to terms with the situation.

Some birthday moms were a wonderful exception. One made small favor boxes with stickers, balls, and beautiful crayons instead of candy. Adrian was deeply moved. He got exactly what the other kids did! Even when Adrian got a bag of candy to take home, he politely said thanks and happily passed it on to his siblings back home.

We eventually discovered that Adrian could have specific types of non-nutritional juices diluted with water. Our specialized dietitian discovered some concentrated icing colors that he could tolerate. For Adrian's birthdays we made colorful ice cubes, slushes and popsicles. He didn't eat much of it, but he loved having something on his plate that he could actually eat if he wanted. The other children observed that he was not upset about not being able to eat hot dogs and chocolate cake, so they weren't bothered, either.

Of course, we ran into weird problems that we could never have prepared for. Like all parents, we were thrilled to see Adrian lose his first tooth. We arranged a "Lost my first tooth party" as we had done for all our children, and we celebrated this milestone. But when no new tooth surfaced, we started to wonder. Now what? We studied Adrian's teeth and discovered much to our surprise that the new tooth was still well preserved within the gum. Because he didn't eat, there was no friction to force the tooth through the gum. Instead, the gum just pushed further forward until it covered most of his baby teeth. What on earth were we to do? The dentist suggested stimulating the gums somehow, but Adrian had developed a strong aversion to having objects in his mouth. Everything tasted, and by now he had become overly sensitized to flavor.

We got some products from the pharmacy intended to help a small teething baby. Key word for these products: baby. None of these aids were intended for an older boy with a considerably stronger bite. Adrian chewed the products to pieces, yet the tooth remained well preserved within the gum. The pharmacist suggested that I might want to visit the pet shop to see if they had any toys for needle-sharp puppy teeth. I snorted and left, however, because I refused to ever serve my kid nylon puppy bones or chewing ropes!

We massaged the gums, but it was no use. The tooth would not surface. Finally, Adrian sat and bit off pieces of raw carrots. He chewed them forcefully and spit out the mass in an Emisis basin. He would rinse his mouth with water and spit it out in the basin. Over and over he repeated the procedure while the tooth worked its way out. It hurt, and he cried while hanging over the carrots and the basin. Afterward, we had to give him IV analgesics all through the night. The gums would get heavily inflamed, and he got a terrible ache in his mouth and jaw. But the next day, he started all over again with the carrots. He continued until finally one day we could feel the saw-edged enamel of the new tooth. He had to go through this every time he was getting a new tooth.

Food may have been important to Granny, but more than anything, she treasured the fellowship it represented. Adrian was just like her. The fellowship of the family was inexpressibly important to him. Spending time together was everything. We, his parents, felt the same way. Because we knew time was a scarce resource, it was infinitely precious to us. We cherished the good moments and wrote them down. Capturing the instant and attaching it to paper became our way of reminding ourselves of what we were grateful for. This turned into many memories and magical moments, collected in seventeen books standing in Adrian's bookshelf. Israel constructed altars of stone to remind each other of what God had done. But stone altars don't fit that easily on a bookshelf.

Winter 2003

After every emergency, Adrian's condition took a turn for the worse. He got tired more easily and had to sleep for several hours during the day. Even during calm periods, weeks and months without any emergencies, we observed how he weakened. He gradually endured less. If he had been able to climb the ladder of the slide, he would have to lie down at the top to rest before being able to slide down.

He could still spend two or three hours in the kindergarten thanks to the efforts of a beautiful human being who assisted him all day. This teacher was able to see Adrian for who he was and adapt every plan to his ever-changing condition.

Throughout Adrian's childhood, we have been blessed with angels who have facilitated our daily life. They made the good even better and the painful easier to carry. The wonderful doctor and the unique kindergarten teacher were two of these people. Our life would have been very different without them.

After some time, it became apparent that Adrian's muscles were deteriorating. He gradually got more exhausted. An occupational therapist who held a temporary position in our local community came to visit and told us that it was about time for us to get a wheelchair for Adrian and to make our house accessible for him. We shrugged and shook our heads in disbelief, but because she was so competent and friendly, we chose to listen to her. The wheelchair arrived six months later. By then, Adrian was so weak that we had to carry him whenever we went outdoors. This was just another example of God sending people our way to bless us. Soon an indoor chairlift for disabled people was assembled to ensure Adrian's access to the second floor.

At the same time the social services determined that Adrian's situation was now "constantly inconstant" and that Thomas no longer qualified for the financial aid that he had been receiving. Social services stated that Thomas should go back to his ordinary job and that nurses from the local community should care for Adrian. Of course, we were not going to leave Adrian's care with anyone else, and the hospital declared that it was of the essence that the parents were in charge of Adrian's care, especially due to his immune deficiency. We knew for sure that there was no way to cope with our daily situation unless both parents could contribute to Adrian's medical care, and we knew we couldn't possibly manage on one paycheck only. It was obvious that Thomas would be unable to comply with his ordinary job combined with the massive workload he already carried in our family.

We invited the bureaucrat from social services to attend a meeting with us and all the other professionals who attended to Adrian's needs. We wanted the bureaucrat to have access to question all the experts. Hopefully, that would lead to a more accurate understanding of Adrian's unique situation and preferably also to more flexibility and benevolence.

"These parents work day and night, executing specialized medical care in their home," the doctor stated. "They should not be getting the reduced financial aid they are currently receiving— they should be getting way more!"

The case officer from the social services sat next to me. I was happy to see her take notes as the doctor described everything we were doing on a regular basis. Finally she would understand— wouldn't she? As she moved her hand, I could see just what she had put down on her notepad. "The doctor says that these parents should not be getting the financial aid that they are currently receiving." Period. Nothing further. She did not take any further notice of what the doctor was saying.

It was the start of a three-year-long battle with the Norwegian legal system. Social services removed our financial aid for ten months while the legal issues were being settled in court. From one month to another, we continuously had to consider whether we could pay our mortgage and for how long we could delay paying our bills without risking going on to debt collection. I reminded myself of what had happened during the early stages of the medical examination and reached the conclusion that I could not possibly have explained in depth how very ill Adrian actually was. I spent countless hours writing in detail everything we did daily just to keep Adrian alive and how crucial it was for us to continue doing so. The answer I got from social services was not to take this personally and that the intention on their part was to settle an ongoing legal controversy on the issue of whether the state or the local community should pay for the medical care of patients who were treated at home. Official authorities chose to use our situation as leverage when entering a legal mine field, and we were left to pay the costs by having Thomas' income revoked for ten months. I am sure that the social services did not mean it to be personal, but it sure felt like it as we were sitting in the dark of the night discussing where we were to live next month.

We won the legal battles, and Thomas was awarded the financial aid that he had previously received. It felt so pointless to waste time and energy on this while our son gradually got weaker. However, we felt vindicated when we realized that our case formed legal precedence for several similar cases, making it easier for them to win in court. We did not want anybody to have to go through what we had been through.

Life was about to change. It became very apparent to us that

I HAVE A GOOD LIFE

Adrian was taking a turn for the worse, and both the physiotherapist and the doctors declared that his muscles were weakening before disappearing.

———————————

A drian was four years old when he was sat in the backseat of the car and asked me the following question:

"If God *can* heal me, and he doesn't *want* to – then what kind of a god is he?"

It would have been easy to rush in and answer with some of the many more or less successful analogies that I have ever heard preached. "Oh yes, God can and he wants to, but sometimes he closes a door in order to open a window." Maybe I could have followed with a sermon on how red light means no, yellow light means wait, and green light means keep going. Finally I could have topped the misery with a few phrases on how maybe God intended for Adrian to be sick so others could get saved. I could have used one of many chewed-up clichés that are repeated so many times they are left with no sense or purpose.

But who is this God who can and will, but who does not heal a seriously ill four-year-old boy who loves Jesus beyond understanding? What kind of God is he?

So I did the only thing I could do. I didn't say anything. I stopped the car at the side of the road and we cried together. We cried for the pain and the difficulties, for the shattered dreams and the mortal blows, for fragile hopes and quivering faith, for disappointments, doubts, scars and wounds of war. We agreed that we did not understand this, and that we never would. It was too vast for our understanding. But both of us felt the presence of God in our lives. His being was there in the car. In our grief. In our longing.

T he second I opened my eyes in the morning I felt the migraine. The visual disturbance was so severe that I needed help to find my way to the bathroom. It had been like that every day for a month. The migraine, which had previously bothered me two to three times a year, had become a daily, uninvited guest.

My body gave in. I could no longer take the night shifts for Adrian. After three years, we had come to realize that we needed to regroup our strength. We reached that awareness a bit too late, as we were empty and exhausted.

Most parents who have seriously ill children find themselves entering into the medical care situation thinking that the disease is temporary. It's just a question of manning up. The doctors will figure out what is wrong, and then we'll just have to fix it. The doctors are so competent, and medical science has come so far. These phrases are repeated incessantly as the only alternative to surrendering to lack of sleep and overwhelming worries. If we for once didn't enwrap ourselves in these banalities, then others would make sure we did. What else could they say? We switched between taking hold of every comforting word with both hands, to receiving the very same words with a disarming smile and polite phrases to make them feel better.

How do you keep on standing when everything is chaos? When you haven't slept for as long as can be remembered, and the body feels like a walking bruise? We kept on reminding ourselves that we were in a state of emergency, but told ourselves it would eventually get better. It surely had to get better. It couldn't remain like this forever—could it?

We stepped on the gas pedal; any lack of progress would not be our fault. We did anything and everything for our son to get well. We came prepared to appointments, constant exams, countless meetings and invading interviews with authorities from the state and the local community. Whenever Adrian was in bed for the night and we had have a couple of hours before he usually would wake up with severe pain, we sat down in front of the computer for our next task—writing the many letters and reports that social services and other agencies demanded in order to comply with urgent needs. We just had to keep going; it had to be done, and beside, it was only for a limited period of time, right? It would have to get better. The most important thing was for our son to be as comfortable as he possibly could be. We would have given anything to achieve that. And so we did.

We managed our energy as if we were running a race of 100-meter hurdles. Full concentration, explosive start, max effort over the hurdle, ignore the lactic acid, and live with the taste of blood in your mouth. Hang in there. Give everything. You can always do better. Just a little more. But after three years of 100-meter hurdles, we realized that we were in the middle of a marathon and probably weren't even halfway yet. What were we to do?

We asked for more medical nurses for the night shifts. We realized that if we were to provide Adrian the attention he needed in the daytime, we had to sleep once in a while. We were met with understanding, but of course it would have to be discussed. Then ads would have to be placed. Then there was the screening process. Followed by the interviews. And then someone might actually get hired. From the moment we asked for full coverage of medical staff for the night shifts until we actually got it, another four years had passed. Another hurdle. Just a little more. Hang in there.

We were still in charge of all sterile procedures and medication, and we wanted it to remain like that. The hospital agreed with us; this was the safest manner due to the immune deficiency Adrian suffered from, and we were not wiling to risk his health unnecessarily. As long as our own health could take it, we wanted to administer the medical care ourselves. We just had to manage. There were many hurdles left.

We never got into the comfortable pace of the marathon. There were just too many medical emergencies, too many unforeseen complications, too much illness amongst the night shift nurses, and way too many unpredictable night shifts for temp nurse, Thomas. We were extremely grateful for our nurses; especially those who made an effort to get to know Adrian well. They contributed to his safety and quality of life, and they have been such a joy to our family.

Some of our friends were patient. Others folded. It became too difficult to relate to a family constantly being in some stage of crisis. They waited for us to put this disease behind us and to move on with our lives. It was tiresome for them to be a part of our unstable existence. That was not what they needed, and we had to accept that.

Others chose a more shallow approach as they asked us how we were doing while studying their watches. We memorized phrases such as "We're OK! There's no emergency going on, so we're happy!" Or "Oh well, it's pretty much the same as always. Isn't it like that for all of us?" It was true; there was no emergency. No immediate change to report, not in any direction. The brilliant smile I got in return revealed the relief of that person. It also assured me that I had estimated correctly as to how much the person in question could cope with. It was not only the concern for the person in front of me that motivated my approach. I simply couldn't stand hearing yet another time, "But have you tried health food? It absolutely changed my life!" Each time I had to choke a sarcastic answer like, "No, we haven't. Why didn't we think of that? I am sure that everything will be different from now on!" In my mind this statement was always followed by a knowing gesture resembling a smack on my own forehead. Both the line and the gesture remained safely guarded in my mind, but sometimes I paid too dearly to keep them in there. We learned to stay away from the people who drained us of much-needed energy.

We were ever so grateful for the ones who endured our situation, who chose to be a part of our life, in the blessings as well as in our worries. Some of them even expressed gratitude for getting to walk alongside us! We are so very, very grateful for those who coped with having appointments cancelled due to some unforeseen issue; who handled us being worn down or empty and who invested in lifting us; who walked with us for an extra mile or fifteen. These fantastic people cheered with us whenever there was a reason, or sobbed uncontrollably with us in the dark seasons.

There are many ways to roll up one's sleeves, many opportunities to get one's hands dirty. Very few can cope with living like that over time. Even fewer choose to do so in order to bless someone. We loved them, simply loved them. They enriched our lives.

"Who are you? Why don't you care??"

I yelled toward the sky between sobs. I was alone in the house; nobody could hear me. Except for the one who ought to. If he wanted to.

"How can you let him be in so much pain? What did he ever do to deserve this? Nothing! He loves you, and still you allow him to go through this much pain! What kind of god are you?"

I howled; I was furious. There I was, in my home office, facing the windows and screaming out everything I was keeping inside.

"Don't ever think that you're getting away with it! Aren't you almighty? So why don't you intervene? If you can save Adrian, but you choose not to, I will hold you accountable! Do you hear me? I am holding you accountable!! I am holding you accountable for the life of my son! We gave him to you. He is your responsibility! Do you hear me? I shall not forget this! I am holding you accountable!!"

Had God, Father Almighty, been physically present in the room, I would have hit him. That's what I felt like, anyway. Instead, I screamed out all my pain and verbally pounded on his chest. I knew he could take it. Just as I knew how important it was for Adrian to express his anger and grief, I knew that my Papa God would contain me. He could take me.

I yelled until I was empty. The hysterical sobbing was over; I was left in my office chair with my feet on the desk. The tears were still running down my face, but I was out of words. In the silence that followed, I could hear God speaking to me, not as a whisper, not in images, but in a clear, audible voice. I got to ask all my questions, and he answered every one of them. The conversation flowed as easily as if I had been talking to Thomas. He reminded me of his promises to me. I felt myself calming down. I remember repeating over and over:

"But I will hold you to this, God. I am holding you accountable. He is your responsibility. I am holding you accountable. I will be reminding you of this."

Then I got up, splashed some cold water on my face and went to meet my children. The responsibility was placed where it belonged.

A WIN-WIN
SITUATION

I froze when I saw the blood on the bedsheets. There was no reason for Adrian to bleed... unless the central intravenous line was broken. I looked under his t-shirt and found the torn catheter poking out.

Fourteen hours earlier we had landed in Málaga, Spain. This was our first trip abroad with Adrian in many years. We were so completely exhausted and were desperate to get some rest. Adrian had been healthy, as in without any infections, for a few months, and the doctor had cleared us to travel. We were so excited and happy to experience something new with Adrian. Well, we did somehow.

In the split second when I saw the torn catheter, adrenaline kicked in. I ran to find the artery forceps that had been waiting in my purse for three years and closed the catheter. Thomas rushed down to the hotel front desk and asked them to call for an ambulance. We were happy to be fluent in Spanish and thus easily understood.

Adrian was pale and shaking with fear. He knew that a torn catheter equaled an opened vein, and that there was only a short distance to his heart. What would happen? He had had an intravenous catheter for three years and was well aware of the risk of infection. I switched between comforting him and talking on the phone to the medical staff of the air ambulance. The situation was completely surreal. More than anything I felt like throwing the phone against the wall so I could just take care of Adrian, but once again I was trapped in this conflict between being a mom and a nurse. This role of professionalized parenting was wearing down my soul.

Eventually it became clear that none of the doctors at the children's hospital had any competence as far as permanent intravenous lines were concerned, although several of them were worryingly willing to operate. One of the doctors suggested that maybe he could weld a urine catheter onto the broken intravenous line so we could continue our holiday. Of course, that was completely out of the question. We soon realized that we had to get Adrian home, and our doctors in Norway cooperated with the air ambulance and the insurance company to transport us home as quickly as possible. In the meantime, we had to wait.

We were placed in the post-anesthesia care unit, a huge hall where the children lay in beds placed in the shape of a horseshoe surrounding a desk where two nurses were stationed. It became apparent that it was not common for parents to stay with their children in the unit, because no other parents were present in the room. We had to argue to ensure that one of us would be allowed to be present with our son, and the nurse locked the door behind us so no one else could enter.

Adrian was given antibiotics intravenously following the instructions from his doctors in Norway. He did not have any pain, but he was still very frightened. We talked continuously, processing what had happened.

In the bed next to Adrian was a little African boy. He seemed to be Adrian's age, about four years old. I overheard a conversation between the nurses and understood that the little boy had been in a car accident and that both his knees were crushed and needed surgery. His parents had also been severely hurt in the accident and had been taken to a hospital for adults. The nurses talked quietly among themselves, saying that he could not have surgery without the consent of the family, and that they needed the signature of the boy's relatives. That could take some time given that they had to travel from North Africa.

From time to time he woke up and cried desperately. I talked quietly to comfort him. He didn't seem to understand Spanish. It was just as well, really, because before long a nurse came over and said with a commanding voice:

"Now, remember that you are a little man, and men do not cry."

I was mortified. As soon as she was gone I whispered eagerly: "Yes, they do! Just cry!"

Adrian felt so badly for the little boy lying there in the bed next to his. He could not possibly imagine what it would be like to lie there, hurt and scared, without his parents present. He cried silently and then started to sing a Norwegian lullaby. The sobbing from the little boy gradually stopped. He lay still while listening and eventually fell asleep. Each time he woke up crying, Adrian would sing to him until he went back to sleep. This continued for as long as they were both in the post-anesthesia care unit. They were two peers with completely different stories.

We were told that the air ambulance was on its way, and we prepared ourselves to leave. It was awful to leave the little boy, but we felt slightly better when we learned his relatives were expected to arrive shortly.

The ambulance took us to the private airport, and we were told to wait in a small building until the aircraft landed. Thomas had picked up our belongings from the hotel room and returned the rental car and was now waiting with us at the airport. While we waited, he spotted a little lizard hiding behind the soft drink machine. Adrian was thrilled to see it. In the midst of all the disturbing things we were experiencing, this was a magical moment.

Twenty-six hours after arriving in Málaga, we left, this time in an air ambulance. It was the shortest holiday ever. We had been so tired and in need of a vacation. Now we got to experience feeling even more exhausted. We practically collapsed as we entered the aircraft and fell asleep before giving it another thought.

The hospital in Norway was prepared for Adrian when we arrived. Everybody had heard of our horrible holiday, and we were put in an isolation unit as we had been hospitalized abroad. We joked about how we expected to be served umbrella drinks and treats—after all, this was our holiday!

Adrian's doctor came in to examine him. Adrian was pale and exhausted, but happy to be in a familiar environment.

"That was quite a holiday," commented the doctor. "What happened in Spain, Adrian?"

He beamed at her: "We saw a lizard at the airport! It was amazing!"

How very typical of Adrian. Comforting others who were scared and in pain, because he knew how they felt. Rejoicing over life instead of grieving over the holiday that went down the drain. Cheering at the small things, because it is better to light a candle than to curse the darkness.

My hero. Our role model.

That Christmas we hung another ornament on our Christmas tree—a small aircraft made of glass. We knew that we had reason to be grateful.

O ur little boy was always smart and thoughtful. He inherited dyslexia from his daddy and an interest for literature and language from his mommy. At the intersection of the two, a magical combination emerged, full of verbal joy and a dedicated commitment to words and constellations. He spoke incessantly, much to his mother's amusement and his father's amazement.

Adrian loved listening to audiobooks. As he usually woke up at 5 a.m., he lay listening to audiobooks for a couple of hours before the day officially had begun. He listened to whatever we downloaded to his iPod, whether it was Winnie the Pooh when he was little, or Sophie's World, as he got older. He wanted the Bible, philosophy, exciting tales, and poetry on his playlists. When we entered his room in the morning, he often smiled, pointed at the headset and waved goodbye to us. He was busy.

He was passionately consumed with words, their origin, and how they logically were connected. He was only four years old when he slightly absent-minded exclaimed:

"I just love foreign words! I use them adequately, too!"

In the very next moment, he was playing with Legos and Playdough with his friends. The fact that adults surrounded him every day might have affected his language, but for the most part he was like other children. One difference is that he may have thought more than other children, as he was awake several hours every night.

One morning he sat upright in his bed waiting for me with

the iPod in his hand.

"Listen to this," he said as he handed me the iPod. The track from Sophie's World was dedicated to Darwin and his theory of evolution, and it dawned on me why Adrian was so upset. "So I'm a burden, am I?" he shouted. "So I should have died because there are things that I can't do and because I'm sick?"

His eyes teared up, and so did my mother's heart. I got him on my lap, and then we talked about what truly gives value to human beings: that we are created in the image of God and meant to live in fellowship with him. I reminded him of how much he was loved, and how very precious he was. We agreed that the real test of whether the fittest deserved survival was how well one managed to take care of the people in need of help, and how poor this society would be without people who added originality and a different perspective.

Adrian calmed down on my lap. Then he said, "Hey Mom, you would probably have died instantly, considering how nearsighted you are. You wouldn't have been able to see a thing without your glasses!"

We laughed and agreed that it was a good thing that Mommy would be granted a chance after all.

He played on while I was left to think of one of the doctors who had greeted us at the hospital one of the many times Adrian had been admitted urgently. With great confidence he declared that if it were his decision, these children should not have received any medical treatment. The cost for the society was unacceptably high, he stated. We ignored him, mostly because he was not involved in Adrian's treatment. But in my mind, I reckoned that the society would pay a huge cost for having a doctor like him employed at the children's ward.

The first day of school was drawing nearer, and we were anxious to find out how that would work out for our little boy. Most parents and children await the first day of school with mixed emotions, but our nervousness seemed justified. Would he manage to stay in school? How would he react to being a part of a class? Would his immune system cope with his being surrounded by 500 students at the local school?

We started planning 18 months before he was due to start school. Our excellent kindergarten teacher contributed, detailing everything that would have to be in place for Adrian to function at school. The headmaster at the time and the inspector met us with kindness and commitment. They planned how to adapt classrooms and surrounding areas, and planned the makeup of the classes for the benefit of Adrian and the other students.

As with all other parents, we proudly took photos of our son on his first day at school. The photos of Adrian show a tired boy lying down, resting on his desk. He was happy—and completely exhausted. After days, weeks and months, both the school and our family realized this couldn't go on. Sometimes he was floored just from the short drive from our house to the school. It was obvious that he was spending more energy than he could afford. Adrian often had to stay at home because he was worn down and exhausted. He had to stay in bed and get intravenous analgesics. It became apparent that this was too hard for him.

The school provided a teacher that came to our house to teach

Adrian. Now and then we tried to take him to school, especially if they had planned extraordinary activities. On a picture from a Christmas event he is lying pale and exhausted in his wheelchair, resting. The wheelchair is parked at the end of the line of students that are onstage singing for the parents.

The other students were encouraging and did their best to include Adrian, and he was happy for visits and birthday invitations. At a parents' meeting, I explained that one of his parents would have to stay with Adrian at the birthday parties.

"Please let me know if I can do anything to help," I said, "it's actually a lot easier for Adrian to bring his mom along if I'm contributing to the party!"

On of the weary dads who just got off from work suddenly woke to life and yelled: "You're welcome to do the dishes!"

All the parents laughed, and one by one they yelled that I would be welcome to their house to do the dishes any time. No need to limit the offer only to birthdays! Again we got to see how information and presence contributed to a sense of security for children and adults, even when facing serious illness and obvious limitations.

After some time birthday parties became too difficult. Within fifteen minutes of arriving at the party, Adrian would sit pale and exhausted, begging Daddy to take him home. This was a loss for Adrian—he felt sad not to be able to join his peers anymore. He picked two students from his class with whom he kept in touch. These were lovely boys who managed to pace themselves so Adrian could manage to keep up with them as they were playing. The two buddies meant a lot to Adrian, and he continued to attend their birthdays. This was a choice Adrian made, himself, even though he knew that he would be bedridden for several days after the parties. We let him be in charge of those decisions. If it was so important to him that he was willing to pay such a price, then we wanted to make sure that we enabled him to participate.

A teacher came to our house for two hours every day and accommodated the teaching to his current condition. He was at the same level as his peers in most subjects, but struggled to achieve good reading skills. We soon realized that his problems were far more comprehensive than could be explained by a diagnosis of dyslexia. He, who had been able to read even before starting school, suddenly discovered that his disease had taken a new turn. He forgot the letters.

At an earlier stage, we had observed how his illness affected his memory. For instance, the number seven was gone for three years. He had no problem understanding the amount, but nevertheless the number seven was completely erased from his vocabulary. He could easily make himself understood by either writing or talking about *the number after six but before eight*, but the word seven itself was gone from his universe. Then, all of a sudden, after three years it came back, without any kind of stimulation or training. His brain had taken on a life of its own, and not all of it was subject to his will.

At times, maybe twice a week, he had to learn the letters all over again. He would get frustrated and annoyed, because he knew he had known this last week! Sometimes he exclaimed, "I don't get why I can't do this! I'm a smart kid!"

He didn't remain sorry for long. He knew that this was a result of his illness and that it didn't reflect his identity. Most of the time he just stayed focused on the task and worked relentlessly.

All words in sequences were hard for him to remember. Days of the week. Months. Rhymes. The multiplication table. It was easier to multiply and calculate than to learn sequential numbers by heart. Names were impossible to learn. (But then again, some of that was due to hereditary disposition from both sides. We can't blame the illness for everything!)

Every subject he perceived to be meaningful remained stuck in Adrian's memory. He repeated each story he heard with impressive details. He loved to learn.

From time to time he forgot people, even the ones who had been important to him. At one time he got a visit from his lovely teacher from the kindergarten. She was sad to learn that Adrian didn't recognize her. He treated her as a kind stranger, but nothing suggested that he knew who she was. Not even as we explained did he manage to recollect memories from the kindergarten. Six months later she came back to visit. He ran happily towards her and started telling her a story that we didn't recognize about a little girl on a farm. We were puzzled by this, but realized that the teacher had tears in her eyes. It was a story that she had told Adrian when he was approximately three years old. All of a sudden, the memories were back. Because she endured and came back, she got to experience a magical moment.

Adrian was exhausted after the daily two hours of school, but we were determined to make use of the time. We didn't know how long he would be able to learn, or how his disease would progress. As homeschool finished every morning, he immediately fell asleep from the exhaustion for at least a couple of hours. We worked closely with his teachers and became specialists at interpreting his condition. On a good day, the teacher might be able to get through all that she had planned and more. On a bad day, he lay on the couch as she read to him. That was all he could manage. Capturing the moments was essential.

"You will receive a letter in a few days. You are being summoned to a meeting with the department of Children's Protective Services. We have received a letter of concern about your son, Adrian."

I sat in the car with my mouth open. I could barely make sense of what the woman said. A letter of concern? For Adrian? I didn't understand. My mind went into slow-motion mode, and it took a few minutes until I was levelheaded enough to ask who had sent the letter expressing their concern, and on what grounds. That she did not know. The letter was sent anonymously. We would be informed of the reasons for the concern at the meeting. It was clear that the woman on the other end of the line wanted to hang up. Apparently, she did not want to talk to me.

I was left speechless. What had happened? Could this be a mistake? Maybe she was trying to reach someone else? Then again, she had mentioned Adrian. Was this really happening?

Through many years as foster parents we had learnt a thing or two about good parenting. We had done many courses and training sessions, and had been through countless hours of individual counseling as well as group sessions. In addition to that, Thomas and I had co-labored together for years because of the special situation in our family, and we were very coordinated as to how we wanted to take care of our children. We knew for sure that we had provided Adrian with nothing but the best care and attention.

So why would anyone send a letter of concern? Thomas was just as shocked as I was, and the hours went by excruciatingly slowly toward Monday when we finally received the letter from Children's Protective Services. It was a formal letter stating that we were summoned to a meeting with Children's Protective Services and the time of the meeting. No reason, no information. The meeting was scheduled two weeks later.

Something happens to you when you wait for such a meeting. Your brain spins out of control as you try to find a logical explanation for the inexplicable. One wonders who would set in motion such an anonymous smear campaign. The woman from CPS implied that the author of the letter apparently had detailed knowledge of our family. That shocked me even more. Anyone who had such knowledge of our family would know that Adrian was treated well. I ended up mentally going through an imaginary list of all the people I knew. Who would want to hurt us? I could no longer sleep, and the days seemed to never end.

We had to inform all the people we cooperated with of the fact that we were subject to an investigation, and that there was a possibility that CPS would contact them to see if there were grounds for concern. Doctors, teachers, and other professionals were upset on our behalf—they thought it was unfair that we should have to experience something like this.

After some time we were allowed to get a copy of the anonymous letter. It stated that the sender was concerned by the fact that Adrian did not attend the local school with the rest of his class. The sender did not take into consideration the fact that he was too sick to go to school and that teachers from the very same school taught him daily in our home. The author of the letter opinioned that he should be participating in ordinary classroom teaching and that we as his parents were neglecting him by letting him be taught at home.

When I read that, my overwhelming sense of impotence gave way to fury. I was livid. When the day of the meeting finally arrived, I was so angry that I was almost eager for the opportunity to meet with CPS and give those people a speedy introduction into life in the real world.

The two young girls who met us at CPS opened the meeting by saying, "Well, as you know we have received a letter of concern. One is concerned with how you care for Adrian. So maybe you could just go ahead and tell us what it is that you're doing?"

We declined. They had asked us to come, and so they would have to tell us what we were or were not doing. No, they weren't able to say, because they weren't actually the ones that had initiated this case. OK. We were willing to wait for the person in charge of the process to join us. The two young ladies informed us that all the leaders were attending another meeting, so there wouldn't be anybody available to inform us as to why they had chosen to open an investigation. Thomas and I looked at each other and decided that we had plenty of time. We could wait until the leaders' meeting was over.

Within minutes, a leader appeared. He explained that they had chosen to open an investigation because we were a foster home, and they wanted to ensure that all our children received excellent care. The fact that CPS had access to countless reports routinely made by external consultants, all of them stating just that, had apparently not crossed their minds. Nobody had cared enough to go through the numerous reports that were sitting in a file cabinet a couple of floors underneath them. Instead, they chose to open an investigation towards the parents.

"OK," we said. "We will tell you what it is like to be the parents of a child like Adrian." With calm voices, we began telling the story of a child unable to eat and who lived on intravenous nutrition only. Of an active boy who was constantly losing abilities and who would get incredibly exhausted. Of a wise and reflective child who observed all the changes in his own body without being able to do anything to stop the negative development. We told them about how he talked about what he would like to do *if* he grew up. We spoke of countless stays in hospitals, of how we would always take him home as soon as possible. We talked about how we would go round the clock to nurse him in order for him to stay at home and not have to remain at the hospital. Tears ran down my face as I explained what it was like to live in a constant state of emergency, ready in case the temperature rose or his general condition worsened. We told them of everything we did to make sure that we could be together as a family, and how we made sure that our children would grow up together as siblings in the comfort of a family. Of what it was like to be the family of a very sick child and his siblings. Of how we ensured that all our children were safe, had predictability, and had a good quality of life.

After a while, none of the three employees made eye contact anymore. They fixed their stare on the desk in front of them. The leader cleared his throat before saying that it could very well be that they decided not to go any further in this matter, but that they would get in touch with us at some point. The meeting was over.

Several months later, we got a letter from CPS. They had found no grounds for concern and were closing the case. No excuse, no apology. No response to the anonymous author of the letter who blindly projected unfounded claims and accusations.

We had spent energy that we did not have on nonsense. Stupidity. False accusations with no roots in reality. Our daily life took a huge toll on us, and we really needed that energy. Instead, we had been robbed of strength and trust.

Four years later, we learned through unofficial channels exactly who had sent the letter of concern. When I first heard the name, I didn't realize who it was. It took some time before it dawned on me and I remembered a woman who attended the same course that we had attended five or six years earlier. I recalled her vaguely. What I remembered about her was that she had been sitting in the living room at the center, bragging about how she herself had sent at least 25 anonymous letters expressing her concern. "It is way better to send 100 too many than one to few," she said as she smiled and continued knitting.

I don't understand how I didn't realize that it was her work, but she was so remote from our life and so completely estranged from real life that it didn't occur to me she was behind this. Meanwhile, I had rummaged through all our friends and all our acquaintances, searching for the one who was out to destroy us. For a long time I could not trust anyone. I could not relate to anybody. I was hurt and in pain. We, who cooperated closely with so many professionals and who relied on mutual trust in our relations with so incredibly many people, became skeptical and searched for hidden agendas. Whenever somebody asked us how we were, we asked ourselves why they would want to know. How were they planning to use whatever information we provided them with? How could we trust anybody?

We had laid down everything to make sure that our children were fine. How could anyone accuse us of neglecting Adrian? If even our best was to be accused, how could we possibly invite people into our weakness?

It took years for the wounds to heal. We learned something about how evil and ignorance sometimes enjoy each other's company. They continuously search for attention and hardly care if anyone gets hurt. Sometimes they knit.

Fall 2008

The best conversations usually took place in the car. Adrian sat quietly and looked out the window, and all of a sudden his thoughts came out in bits and pieces.

"It's a win-win situation," he murmured.

I smiled. I was used to him pondering words and phrases, and he was at it again.

"What is a win-win situation?" I asked while checking the rearview mirror.

He looked at me absentmindedly and met my gaze in the mirror.

"I cannot lose," he said.

I could tell from the expression on his face that he was still occupied with his own thoughts. I drove on while waiting for him to be ready to share them with me. From time to time, I watched him in the mirror. He was in in his regular seat in the back of the car. Behind him, the electric wheelchair was parked. Because his muscles had weakened, he could no longer sit up straight in an ordinary car seat. He now had a specially adapted car seat that supported his back. It came with tilting options that enabled him to change the pressure point so he would not hurt as much as before. The new car seat in the adapted car had provided us with a new freedom. Adrian no longer cried from pain after ten minutes in a car. Instead, the car rides had come to signify a welcomed opportunity for rest and thought processing.

"I mean, it's impossible to lose. It can't actually happen!"

He woke to life now, and his blue eyes sparkled. I could see that he was literally bubbling with excitement. He leaned forwards in the car seat and hung by the seatbelt while waving his arms enthusiastically. He had realized something.

"If I live, I'm with Jesus. If I die, I'm with Jesus. I win either way!"

I studied him in the rearview mirror. He beamed while he patiently waited for me to understand the implications of what he had just said.

Where did he get this? I knew for sure we had not taught him this. On the contrary, as parents we had often sighed over the fact that we were so easily caught up in the busy routines of daily life that we failed to teach our children Bible knowledge and the foundation of our faith. I knew for sure that he could not have picked this up in church, as I had been writing all the teaching material for the children's ministry for several years. Paul's letter to the Romans had not been part of that material.

So where did he get this everlasting truth from? I looked at how he beamed and knew. He got it from the source.

Quite often we discovered that he had knowledge he naturally should not have had access to. He listened attentively to what others told him before going somewhere to be by himself and ponder it while building with Legos. Often he talked about it once he had it sorted out in his mind, but other times he just stored it on his hard drive without further comment. Once in a while we heard bits and pieces without being able to determine their place of origin, and then we knew that it came from Adrian's own inner life and the continuous dialogue he maintained with the source.

Several times he came from the children's ministry and in a slightly overbearingly manner tell me that in his opinion I should have structured the teaching differently. As he explained why, I often had to acknowledge that he was right.

He loved the stories of Hezekiah. The thought of one man's prayer changing God's plan really impacted him. God allowed Hezekiah to test him—Adrian thought that was just awesome! He liked to study how Jesus met people, and he was very enthusiastic whenever we discussed ethical dilemmas. It seemed that he pretty much knew for himself what he needed to learn. In one occasion he shrugged his shoulders in annoyance whilst murmuring: "In my opinion, you have neglected your duties, Mom. You should have taught me more about King David!"

I used to read to Adrian every night as he went to bed. We read all kinds of literature, although we spent a whole year reading *The Lord of the Rings*, which was our favorite. From time to time, we read from a children's Bible. That was OK, until Adrian started to read himself. Then he came rushing in, dropped the children's Bible on the table with a loud thump, and asked what kind of fake Bible this was. It didn't say a word about Isaiah! He would not bother with such nonsense, thank you very much!

The very next afternoon we went to the bookstore to get a new Bible. It didn't take long before it was filled with notes and markings. The Bible was no theoretical book to Adrian. He recognized the truth when introduced to it.

We realized that Adrian's disease was progressive, which was confirmed by the doctors. He constantly grew worse. His walk became wobbly; he fell often, even after just a few steps. His day-to-day condition varied extremely, something that frustrated him.

"I just don't get it. I could do this yesterday!" he yelled.

We became really good at predicting the development before it occurred and watching out for whatever he needed even before he was aware of it. It might be giving him a hand to discreetly help him get up on the couch, or helping him getting dressed while claiming that we needed a good cuddle. He was overbearing, after all; he thought we were the one's who needed the cuddle. I changed all the small pearls that children used for crafts with bigger ones, stating that the big pearls made for improved trivets whenever melted in the oven. I didn't mention that he could no longer play with the small pearls due to his failing motor skills. Besides, the colors of the bigger pearls were so much nicer! We did not pay attention to the things that he could no longer do—our only focus was the things he still managed. In this way, we reduced the strain of having a progressive disease both for Adrian and for the rest of the family.

It didn't make sense comparing him to his peers—we just compared him to himself. If he managed to do something that he had not been able to do before, the whole family cheered. If he could no longer do something he had mastered before, we searched for alternative solutions among the aids or technical inventions. Thomas used to work with adapting cars for disabled people before we got a sick child and found ourselves sitting at the other side of the table. As Adrian lost motor skills, Dad came up with technical solutions and adaptations.

Adrian got used to focusing on the solution. As ataxia and tremors made it impossible to make crafts even with the bigger pearls, he pushed his elbow towards the ribs while resting his right wrist on the table to regain control of his right hand. The focus was on the task to be solved. As he could no longer draw, he began making wonderful pictures on his computer. Every year he painted glass items to give to grandparents and friends for Christmas. It was important to us to enable him to bless others. We often talked of how we needed to make some deposits in the memory bank, both for our benefit and that of others.

Time is a scarce resource. When conscious of limited time, it becomes imperative to think through carefully how it is spent. It became clear to us that the house we were living in presented limitations to Adrian's life.

Our beautiful old home consisted of four floors. Even with a stair lift between two of them, Adrian's mobility was severely reduced. A stair lift requires someone to get seated and then push a button for the time it takes for the lift to get from one floor to another. Adrian struggled to get seated, and as time went by, it became impossible for him to push the button. Even with continuous adaptations, we had to realize that this solution no longer was sufficient to secure his quality of life. It became obvious the day when Adrian absentmindedly sighed, "Oh, I'm so tired. I wish I could manage to go to my room!"

It hit me in the stomach. It was not like he could not be bothered to go to his room on the second floor—he was not able to. We had exceeded all possibilities for reconstruction of our

60-year-old, traditional Norwegian wooden house. Adapting our house any more than we already had was simply impossible.

We realized that we had to move, but it wasn't as if there was any wheelchair-adapted house ready and waiting for us. We faced a dilemma. Should we build a new house? What if Adrian only had a limited time left to live? Did we really want to spend those last years of his life building a house? What would be the best way to steward the time given to us with Adrian?

We thought about it and prayed, discussed it, and prayed again. Weeks and months went by as we studied possible solutions while paying attention to the housing market. In the end, we concluded that we would have to construct a house. We felt calm after having made the decision.

It was a good thing that we had actually felt peace at some point, because to say that the following years were busy would be an understatement. For anyone to sell a house, build a new one, and move is a hectic process, but try combining that with taking care of a very sick child, handling his IV nutrition and medication, attending all the meetings with the professionals on our support team, and being proactively present in the life of your child. We remained in a state of emergency. Days and nights went into the process of planning a house that would meet all of Adrian's current and future needs. We had to come up with solutions that would accommodate the nurses, the teacher and the homeschooling, storage for devices and IV equipment, cool storage for IV nutrition and medication, elevators and installations, automatic doors and windows—and for Adrian to get to everything in an electric wheelchair with a pretty big turning radius!

We prayed for our new home to be a place where the Spirit of God rested. We prayed that we would get to bless other people. We blessed everyone who helped us in the process of getting the house ready.

Finally it was done, and we could move in. Adrian had turned nine, and he now had his own apartment within the house where he could receive his nurses and the teacher. All the IV equipment was now stored in four-five cubic meter closets in his hallway. The entrance of his apartment was connected to the garage so he could drive his wheelchair straight in from the garage without getting wet or cold. His bedroom was connected to a bathroom to make it easier for him whenever he was hooked up to his IV line. He had a living room where he could go whenever he was tired and needed some space from the rest of our brood.

Adrian flourished. He loved his new independence, and we loved the dignity it provided him. Little by little we realized that we had been given a new freedom, too. We didn't have to escape the kitchen anymore for Adrian to be alone with his teacher. We no longer had to have a night nurse on duty in the room next to our bedroom. We no longer had boxes with IV equipment stacked all over our house because we actually had somewhere to store them. We saw that Adrian had more energy to play and learn now that he no longer had to overcome all the obstacles he was used to facing. We had run up a huge debt, but we were happy to offer this house to Adrian and our other children. To us, it was a gift from God.

For weeks after we moved in, we still had a steady flow of carpenters and others passing through our house to fix the last details. One day I overheard a conversation between Adrian and the electrician. While mounting lights in Adrian's room, the electrician talked about something that had happened to him in Sweden. Adrian said that he had been in Sweden, too.

"Oh yeah? On holiday?" asked the electrician.

"No. In hospital," Adrian said and continued to play with his toys.

"Hmm," pondered the electrician, "Have you been in any other countries?"

"Yes," said Adrian and listed some other countries.

All of a sudden I noticed his voice changing slightly before he continued: "Parts of me have been in other countries, too, such as the Netherlands and England." He maintained a straight face, but the electrician seemed to notice the sparkle in his eye. The electrician thought it over before finally asking whether that had something to do with his staying in hospitals. Adrian smirked as he told him about the different tissue biopsies that had been sent to labs all over the world.

A few seconds passed before the electrician continued: "Hmm. I'm guessing you don't have many memories from those trips."

Adrian was ecstatic! He had met somebody who shared his sense of humor, and he was delighted! He loved pulling pranks on adults, especially if he noticed someone being a bit reserved and serious. He studied the technicians who did the ultrasound of his stomach and evaluated them. Sometimes he stared at them with those huge eyes and ask: "Do you know how to do this? Are you any good? Could you show me my gallbladder, please? I've always wondered what that looks like."

Those who had prepared before coming in and read through his medical history knew well that he had had his gallbladder removed at the age of four and a half due to gallstones. Those who glanced at him instead of focusing solely on the computer might have guessed from the scars on his stomach. But those unprepared and who didn't dignify him with a single glance started to sweat as they failed to identify the gallbladder on the screen. After a while they murmured something about it not always being easy to find before finally asking, "Do you know where your gallbladder is?" Adrian lit up and explained that it was in the bin for biological waste!

You get a weird sense of humor when you are sick for a long time. Maybe we got a bit sick, too, because we loved his humor.

I HAVE A
GOOD LIFE

E ven when living with a seriously ill child, someone is not prevented from other challenges of life. Things happen in your surroundings that you cannot be protected against or avoid. This became apparent during 2010 and 2011, when several things happened in and around our family, leaving us crushed. I cried more during that spring than I ever had in my life. We were heartbroken.

Ties of grief and sorrow came to hold our family ever closer, and a sense of fellowship surfaced that had not been there before. Together we began to long for something else—to experience more of God, more of his presence. Many people prayed for us during this period, and even in the most vulnerable time of our lives we experienced how we were carried through these grief-stricken days.

The Christmas ornament looked different that year. For the first time, we handed over a Bible verse to an artist to make the ornament for us. Isaiah's words of the Holy One who would bring to life our wounded hearts and revive the spirit of the lowly gave us hope that we sometime would feel whole again (Isaiah 57:15). The Christmas ornament showed transparent glass lying shattered on the ground. Above it arose a whole and new red heart. We were grateful for the promise we had been given: that our faithful father would heal what was crushed and broken.

We experienced God in a different way than before. Adrian often saw angels around us, and a little girl who used to spend time with us told her mother that "it was nice to be at Marian and Thomas' place because there were so many angels there." Another guest saw an angel rising towering through all the floors and guarding our house. We never saw these angels ourselves, but we had a strong feeling of protection.

Thomas and I started talking about how we wanted to create a major family project. We needed to do something with our kids to experience something new together and to consolidate our family. We, who had been Christians all our lives, longed to see more of God's greatness.

I felt nausea when I thought about the tame, safe god who had taken center-stage in many of the Christian fellowships. What had happened to the Almighty God, the Creator? Who had tamed Jesus, Lord of life and death? It seemed to me that people felt a need for order, and so a predictable, manageable "god" was more welcome than the Almighty God—because imagine if he did anything to embarrass the church?

Understand this; I love the local church, the close-knit fellowship of searching people. But I love Jesus more. The need for a predictable and safe existence in the church can never be achieved at the cost of the love for Jesus. What he wants is more important to me than the soothing comfort of the church.

I longed for the Jesus that C. S. Lewis knew, the one he outlined in the Chronicles of Narnia: "He is not like a tame lion."

I longed to get blown away by the roar from the lion of Judah. I longed to see what he did and to repeat it myself. The thought of continuing the walk in the desert was out of the question. We wanted to see people touched by the power of God, not by a cozy culture or the comfort of the static.

We decided to go on a journey with our children and combine it with the celebration of our 20th wedding anniversary. Thomas and I first discussed this without the kids being present because we needed to go a few rounds to decide what was best. We couldn't visit any theme parks as Adrian's muscles had weakened so much by then that his body would no longer remain behind the safety bars of rides. They would be way too dangerous for him. We had to think through where we could go, keeping his immune system in mind, and we quickly realized that it would have to be to a country with functioning hospital facilities.

When asking each other what we wanted to do, we both arrived at the conclusion that we wanted to visit a church. During the previous months, we had listened to a lot of worship music, and in particular to Jesus Culture and Bethel Church. Our kids liked the music, too. Could the idea be to visit Bethel Church? We felt ourselves getting excited and happy—this sounded like a brilliant idea! Quick searches on the internet showed that the church was located in Redding in Northern California, which meant it was on the wrong side of the USA from our Norwegian home, considering how many hours of travel Adrian could possibly cope with. This suddenly seemed like the worst idea of all time, so we left it behind.

Then God was silent. We did not hear anything for two months. It certainly was not due to lack of effort—we searched, sought, prayed, and discussed. Silence. We did not sense God's Spirit talking to us in any way. It was time for reflection: When was the last time we heard God and felt his presence? Well, it was when we talked about going to Bethel Church. In a split second, the presence of God was back with us, as concrete as anything else surrounding us. We had to find out more about this church.

How on earth would we get to Northern California? In our global day and age that sounds like one small step for mankind, but for a seriously ill child depending on IV nutrition, it was more of an unimaginable trek.

We studied flights and schedules and calculated traveling for approximately 20 hours. That implied that Adrian would have to be connected to his IV nutrition during the flight to avoid hypoglycemia due to lack of nutrition. We contacted the airlines and travel agencies to find out how we should approach this issue, but none wanted to discuss a hypothetical situation.

That could be easily fixed, we thought, and so we bought tickets to San Francisco. Now that we were no longer discussing a hypothetical journey, we reckoned that the airlines would have to answer us concerning the IV nutrition. Oh blessed ignorance! It turned out to be completely impossible to get the airlines to commit to even considering the issue. We were lost in endless conversations with offices in Norway, Germany, England, and the USA, but nobody wanted to assume responsibility for transporting more than half a liter of fluids onboard the aircraft. Adrian needed to get 2.5 liters of nutrition infused intravenously during 24 hours. Then came the saline solution, intravenous medication, pain relief—a total of approximately 4 liters. That is what he needed onboard to be able to travel to California. He would also have to be connected to two IV infusion pumps. That was no problem, said the lady on the phone, as long as we turned them off during take off and landing. We realized that while it might be difficult for her to understand, we knew that it would be medically irresponsible to turn the IV pumps off for the period she requested.

We spent several months calling the travel agency and several airline companies asking them to guarantee that we would get to board with the IV nutrition. We provided a statement from the hospital, from the specialized pharmacy which produced the nutrition, and from the provider of the IV pumps, ensuring that the equipment we were carrying would pose no threat, and that we as parents were competent to handle any situations that might occur so that no further medical assistance would be required. All the people we talked to on the phone were understanding and friendly. They all promised to get back to us with a clear answer. They never did. It began to dawn on us that we would get no such assurance, and that we would end up standing in the airport without even knowing if we would get to go.

We did whatever we could to make sure that everything would be all right. When we still didn't get the clearances we wished for, we were not all that bothered. God had said that we were going to California, so he would have to see to it, we reasoned. This was his responsibility. We rented a house in Redding to stay in while we participated in a conference in Bethel Church.

After a while, we informed our kids of our plans to travel. The oldest two were thrilled and cheered, while Adrian rested his head on the kitchen table and said seriously, "I can think of at least a hundred reasons why this will never happen."

He knew how much it would take to travel with such an amount of equipment, and how easily some medical situation could occur which would make it impossible to go. We smiled and calmed him down, but it was quite obvious that he was not going to cheer for this, not until he knew that he was actually on his way.

Spring 2012

Our flight tickets stated that we could bring 23 kilos (51 lbs) of luggage each. Excellent, we thought—that means that we get to take 115 kilos (254 lbs)! Packing would be a walk in the park!

That was before realizing how much the medical equipment alone would weigh.

We wrote down every single item we would need to be gone for 16 days. We had to distribute the medical equipment over several suitcases to make sure that we would still have enough equipment if one of the suitcases went missing. Intravenous connection set and tubes, reflux valves and taps, medication and pumps, sterile gloves and surgical masks... Everything was put on the lists because we could not risk forgetting anything. We went over the lists again and again before being ready to pack. Then it was time to weigh the suitcases.

The medical equipment we needed to be gone for 16 days weighed 110 kilos (243 lbs). Which meant that there were precisely five kilos left for all our clothes. We sensed something expensive coming on.

New phone calls to the airline companies. Could we be granted extra luggage for our medical equipment? No surprise—nobody could answer that. OK then, we would just have to pack whatever we needed and meet at the airport. We knew where we were going.

I wish I could have told my kids that everything would be OK and that it was all taken care of. Instead, I remember all too well how difficult even travelling within Norway had been with Adrian hooked up to his IV line. Way too many times we had been asked to take a sip from his IV nutrition to demonstrate that it was not dangerous. Every time we would have to explain that this was a sterile liquid that was being infused straight into our son's veins, and drinking from it would ruin the sterile solution. Each time we would be met with a blank stare before they repeated the request.

I instructed our kids to be quiet as we were due for check-in. The woman behind the counter studied the amount of luggage.

"You sure are taking a lot of stuff!" she said.

"Yep," I answered, "110 kilos (243 lbs) of medical equipment."

She looked at me briefly, asking why we were taking so much, and I explained that that was how much equipment was needed to go on a holiday with a child who needed intravenous nutrition.

"What have you been told to do with this?" she asked.

Thomas answered that we had called countless times, still failing to get a clear answer. She studied the screen of her computer for a long time before giving us our tickets and checking our luggage all the way to San Francisco. We thanked her and walked toward the elevator. The kids started asking questions, but we told them told to be quiet for a little while longer. Once we got inside the elevator, the questions came like an avalanche: "Why didn't we have to pay for the extra baggage? Why didn't we have to pay for having too many items?" We were grateful to have gotten that far—now we braced ourselves for the never-ending questions that remained at the security control checkpoint.

Thomas was supposed to go through with Adrian. The woman in front of them was carrying a small bottle of water that she was told to leave behind, and Thomas and Adrian exchanged glances. Would they even get to board the plane? Dad had forgotten to take off his belt and was stopped in security. In the meantime, the security staff rolled the wheelchair with Adrian in it away. Thomas hurried after them while preparing to explain the huge backpack that was hanging at the back of the wheelchair.

"What is that?" asked one of the guards as he pointed at the spiraled tube that went from the backpack to Adrian's body.

"It's a tube that transports the intravenous nutrition that's in the bag. Would you like to see it?" he said while getting ready to open the backpack.

"No, it's OK," the guard said as he had already moved on. Thomas was left flabbergasted before he came to his senses and the two of them hurried over to the rest of the family. As we rushed on, the words slipped from one of the kids, "What? What just happened? Those people at security didn't see anything. It was as if they were blind or something!"

The security guard standing next to us studied us cautiously, but let us move on. He was right, though. It was as if they were blind. Never before had we experienced so few problems while travelling with Adrian and all his equipment.

At the airport in Germany, the same scenario repeated itself: We got to pass straight through without any tiresome rounds of questions or extra security controls. We had traveled enough with Adrian to know that this would not usually be the case for our family. Ordinarily, we would have been detained and asked so many questions that we would risk missing the plane, but now it was as if the way had been cleared for us, and we could board without any problems. Finally, as the plane left from Germany to San Francisco, Adrian realized that we were actually going on holiday to the USA. All of a sudden, it was as if he sensed a flicker of hope for what lay ahead for him.

T he last six months before our trip, we had spent quite some time listening to the teachings of Bethel. We downloaded podcasts and worked our way through two years of teaching. It dawned on us that they had understood something we still had not gotten hold of.

It was not as if we had never experienced anything with God through all the years we had known him. On the contrary, God felt very present, especially through the years of Adrian's illness. He was great, powerful, comforting and... passive. Of course I realize that belief speaks more about us than God, but that was our experience of him. From time to time, I felt small breezes of his power, especially during worship or through things that my kids said without thinking. Then, all of a sudden, I felt as if giant doors opened over me and I got to feel drops of heavenly rain before the doors slammed shut and I was left outside in the dust. I longed for torrential rain.

I was desperate for more of God. Not necessarily for Adrian to be healed, but because I needed it for myself. Thomas felt the same way. We would not settle for this powerless way of life—we knew we needed more of the Father.

When Adrian was little, we prayed to God for his healing. Often we entered his room at night, laid our hands on him, and prayed for him as he was sleeping. Other times we talked with Adrian about healing and prayer, but left it to him to decide what he wanted. It was important to us that he would not be made to feel inferior for being sick. To us, he was absolutely perfect just the way he was. He did not have to get healed for us to love him.

Many people prayed for Adrian for years. His grandma often told us that she was praying for his healing. I thanked her, knowing that I myself was unable to remain constantly pleading to God. However, it felt good to have someone who could lift our arms toward heaven. I prayed for Adrian to be happy and pain free, but the nursing situation was so demanding that we were forced to be present in our daily life. We could not remove ourselves to get the necessary distance to see things objectively. We did not live with a constant dream of seeing Adrian healed. What we longed for, was for ourselves and our children to get a new encounter with the living God.

A few weeks before our departure, we realized that there were several signs and wonders going on in Bethel Church. We had heard of it before, but had failed to comprehend the extent to which they happened. Many people were healed, and God revealed himself through different manifestations that occurred in the church.

We discussed how to approach this when it came to Adrian. We were open to healing and prayer and had seen people in our surroundings getting healed, but it was important to us for our son not to feel devalued. Because Adrian was in a wheelchair it was quite obvious that something was wrong, and the thought of having him surrounded by complete strangers wanting to pray for him concerned us.

We decided that we would talk to him about it.

"Adrian, quite a few wonders and healings happen in Bethel, and maybe somebody would like to pray for you. What are your thoughts about that?" Our 12-year-old considered this before shrugging, "I don't know. I have a good life."

It is possible to have two thoughts at the same time. On one hand I thought, "What is wrong with you, kid? Don't you want to get healthy?" On the other, I was grateful beyond words. As a mother, it was balm to my soul to hear that my son had a good life, regardless of disease and circumstances.

We had only been in Bethel for a few hours when Adrian leaned over and whispered in my ear, "Mom, now I know that no matter what God has for me, that's what I want. I know that's what's best for me."

In the presence of God everything else fades away.

On the second day of the conference, we participated in a breakout session on healing, and people from the church told us of several miracles that had happened there. I was shaken to my core when I heard of the different healings that could only be explained as the result of a creative miracle. We cheered as we heard of people who had had their lives restored and upgraded, and I could feel my own perception of God changing. As they kept on giving testimonies, I was no longer surprised. Instead, I caught myself thinking: "Of course he did! That's just who he is!"

At the end of the session they asked if anyone needed to get healed. Adrian's hand shot up in the air. I smiled but stayed close ready to assist if needed. Many people wanted prayer. "Keep your hand up for the people around you to see. They are the ones who will be praying for you," they said from the stage. I was happy to see that it was so down to earth, that you didn't have to turn to specific people to get prayer, and that the young man standing next to us was the one who would be praying for Adrian.

He asked what was wrong. Adrian and I looked at each other and decided that we could not possibly mention everything; it would take too long. Instead, I explained that Adrian could not eat.

"OK," he said, "I know what it's like. I, too, had celiac disease."

For a split second, I wondered whether I should elaborate, but quickly came to the conclusion that God would know what the problem was, anyway. He prayed for new life in Adrian's stomach. Adrian smiled and thanked him for praying for him, and then we were leaving. I asked him if he had sensed anything.

"No," he said, "I couldn't feel any difference, but it felt good to be prayed for."

We met the rest of the family and decided to go for a meal. The next meeting was in a few hours, and we were determined not to miss it. We had very little time to get something to eat, so we decided to eat out to save time.

We rushed into an Italian restaurant and ordered quickly. We knew that we would have to get to the church early to get seats as there were usually long lines in front of the doors even an hour and a half before the meeting started. In the middle of the table, there was a glass with grissini: long, thin sticks of bread. Adrian asked if he could have a breadstick, and we hesitated while thinking about how other children might have played with them before putting them back into the glass. Finally we said yes—after all, he was not going to eat it.

Ever since Adrian was very little, he had enjoyed having food on his plate during meals. He liked to dissect the food, as he called it. His mealtime experience consisted of cutting the food into pieces, mixing sauces and ingredients, and enjoying the smell. He could not eat anything without becoming seriously ill. We had tested him several times throughout his childhood. Even as late as a few days before leaving, we had given him a tiny piece of watermelon to see if he could have it. He immediately got sick, so we knew that when it came to eating, nothing had changed. Nevertheless, he enjoyed cooking, smelling the food, and being a part of the social setting at the table.

There was an ongoing buzz at our table at the Italian restaurant. As always, our family shared life and experiences during the meals, and this was no exception. We had experienced so much already during our stay in Bethel. One of our kids had joined others in prayer for a woman who had been born deaf but got her hearing back. Others had seen for themselves that people were getting healed. We had all felt the palpable presence of God, and we could not get enough. We were all talking at once as everyone shared what he or she had experienced.

"Can I have another one?" Adrian asked. We absentmindedly answered that no, he could not, because he already had one.

"Not anymore," said Adrian.

It is impossible for me to describe the feeling I got in my stomach as I turned around and looked at his empty plate. Adrian was sitting there with a sheepish gaze on his face with the rest of the family staring at him. All I could think, was, "Oh no! How does this end?" Thomas was the first to break the silence as he asked, incredulous, "Did you eat it?"

Adrian gave a nod as he wore the same sheepish grin. My voice was slightly more forceful than I had intended it to be as I asked, "Why?"

He really could not say. He had just eaten it. Was he feeling sick? No, he was not—he could not feel any difference, he replied. By the way, could he have another one? The rest of the family in unison yelled: "No!"

Adrian looked slightly disconcerted, but still had the same quizzical grin. It was as if he knew that he should be worried, but he still could not stop smiling.

Thomas and I looked at each other. What were we going to do now? More than ten years had passed since Adrian last ate ordinary food. The tests that he had been through during these years had shown that he still could not digest food, and the examinations at the hospital had proven that he did not have any ability to absorb nutrients in his intestines. What would happen now? We switched to Spanish to buy a little time to talk without the children being a part of the conversation. We were worried and very conscious of the fact that a grissini was not what we would have served Adrian to "test his healing." We agreed that we would give it some time, monitor his general condition, and act accordingly. In the meantime, we were determined to go the next meeting.

We hurried back to the house we had rented and connected Adrian to his daily IV nutrition. His facial color was fine, and he seemed to be in good shape. That is also what he expressed every time we asked him how he was doing, which we did at least 50 times that afternoon. All the time we kept watch of him out of the corner of our eyes, searching for the tiniest sign telling us that we should take him to the hospital, but he was relaxed and showed no sign of pain. We piled the kids and the wheelchair back into the rental van and headed for Bethel Church.

Our favorite part of the meeting was the long time of worship and adoration. It gave us time to clear away stress and worries and just to focus on the one who deserved our attention. An hour and a half of worship went by quickly. Most people were standing, but those who wanted to sit sat down in their seats. Some lay on the floor. Nobody gave it another thought; here, everyone encountered the Father in his or her own way. Our eldest children chose to stand in front of the stage, while we remained standing next to our seats. Adrian lay down on the empty seats behind us. He sang some, read in the Bible, closed his eyes and rested, listened to his audiobooks, and did whatever he wanted to. Whenever he had the strength, he stood on the seat, sloping over my or Thomas' shoulders as we worshipped. Sometimes he put his arms over ours and together we lifted our arms toward heaven. The presence of God was overwhelming and as concrete as anything else surrounding us. After a while, we helped Adrian back to his wheelchair, and he rested as he switched between listening to the worship in the church and listening to the *Lord of the Rings* on his iPod. It was the most blessed mix ever, according to Adrian.

During worship two ladies came over to Adrian and asked if they could pray for him, and he said yes. I began explaining what was wrong with him, but they shook off my explanations. I knew why—at the breakout session earlier that day they had said that they did not want overly detailed descriptions of the problem because it might take away the focus from the problem solver. I understood this and was fine with them praying for him without knowing his medical history. Adrian was connected to IV nutrition, and they got that he had a digestive problem. Because he sat in a wheelchair, they understood that something was wrong with his muscles. That is exactly what they prayed for: a new digestive system and strength in his arms and legs. Amen.

Afterward, one of the ladies gave me a card with her name and e-mail and asked me to inform them of what God had done. It was as simple as that. No trickery, just childlike expectation. They wanted feedback to rejoice with us and to give glory to the Father for what he had done.

Once again, I asked Adrian how he had felt while receiving prayer, and once again, the answer was the same. It felt good, but he had not noticed any difference in his body. That was fine by me. I was just thrilled that he had not become sick from that breadstick.

June 2012

The kids refused to leave the church at night to go home. They dragged out the time to remain in the presence of God for as long as possible. We understood, because we too felt this extraordinarily precious presence. It is too simplistic to say that God is in us, and therefore he is everywhere we are. Of course he is, but in addition to that, we got to experience this palpable, all-consuming presence. It was as if we were dressed in his love.

When we finally got home, it was almost midnight, and we had been in church for five hours. The kids were still snorting with annoyance, without getting the point of going home. The only reason they cooperated even a little with us was the promise of going back to church at 10 a.m. the next day.

This was not an ordinary situation in our family. Our kids had gone to church services for as long as they could remember, but this was the first time I had ever seen them long for more. They had encountered the living God, and all of a sudden, nothing else mattered.

We improvised supper, and once again the conversation was buzzing. All of us had seen firsthand the work of God, and we shared stories of what we had seen and heard. All of a sudden Adrian asked if he could have half a slice of bread. Thomas and I exchanged glances. He had not become sick from the breadstick. Besides, we had learned at Bethel that it was important to test a possible healing. Yes, he could have half a slice of bread.

He crawled into an armchair and balanced the plate in front

of him. I studied him. He had put his legs underneath him and was crouching down with the plate in front of his feet. His eyes sparkled as he studied the half slice of bread. Then he began to pick small pieces of the bread and put it into his mouth. A smile spread all over his face as he happily tasted it. There he was, sitting in his pajama shorts and a t-shirt, feet up in the chair, the plate balancing on his toes, towering over the half slice of bread while eating with his mouth open, smacking his lips loudly. I laughed. He reminded me quite a bit of Gollum as he was sitting there, and he grinned when I told him.

"My precious," he wheezed, "my preciousss!"

We all laughed. Table manners would have to come later. Right now we just wanted to enjoy this wonderful moment.

June 2012

After the children had gone to bed, Thomas and I were left to talk about what had happened. Adrian had eaten! For the first time in more than ten years! What had happened? Was he healed? If so, what had he been healed from? Everything? Or just from something specific? And if so, from what?

At Bethel they often talked about testing the healing. They encouraged everyone who wondered if they had been healed to do something they had been unable to do before. They also strongly encouraged everybody to contact their own doctor to see if the disease was gone. Adrian had definitely tested his healing. He had eaten bread twice! Now we had to wait and see whether he would remain fine or get ill.

We talked about the possible consequences we would face if it turned out that Adrian had not been healed. Would he get sick during the night? But he had tolerated the grissini. What should we prepare for?

We had taken care of Adrian's every need ever since he was a baby. Through all these years with serious illness, we had remained like solid rocks. We had followed up on his IV nutrition and everything related to it, in every detail. We had paid attention to every loss of skill, adapted his surroundings, and made sure he got the equipment he needed. We were used to observing, registering, and acting continuously according to his condition. And now, all of a sudden, we had gone against everything that was normal to us. It was so completely out of character for us as parents to a very sick child. What had we done?

Being responsible and resourceful parents, we tried to imagine what could possibly happen if Adrian got really sick. We really tried to come up with genuine worries, but were unable to. Any attempt at serious concerned frowns gave way to uncontrolled giggling. We were at peace.

When the apostle Paul talks of a peace that surpasses our understanding, he is not exaggerating. There we were, in something that should have been a state of emergency, grinning stupidly. We just could not worry. We knew that God was in control, and that our more or less genuinely felt worry would not make any difference whatsoever. We just had to wait and see.

We remained seated for some time that night, praying. It was not a prayer born out of despair—it was more like chatting with our heavenly Dad. We were so grateful for all that we had experienced and for his wonderful presence. If Adrian were healed, that would be an extra bonus, but the greatest experience was ours already in our encounter with God. Those were not just mere words—it was actually how we felt.

Afterward, we went to bed. We knew that either we would have the worst night ever, or else Adrian had been healed. We went to sleep.

Adrian slept all through the night, and so did we. The next morning we woke up before him, and we hardly dared look at him to see if he was still alive. He slept peacefully in his bed, rosy-cheeked, and it was obvious that he was pain-free.

He woke up and looked at us. Within seconds he asked for breakfast. We were ecstatic over the fact that he had slept through the night without any pain—it felt like a miracle. We disconnected him from his IV line and sent him to the bathroom. We went to the kitchen to prepare the long-awaited breakfast.

We hardly got to the kitchen before hearing a roar. It was the sort of noise that makes you react before you even know what you are reacting to. We ran toward the sound and stormed into the bathroom where Adrian was at the toilet. He was desperate and inconsolable while explaining that something was happening that was way past his control.

It took a few seconds before we were able to mentally process what was happening. Adrian had suffered from diarrhea his whole life, and now he was about to lay his first solid cable ever. He was in shock! He did not realize what was going on, nor did he have enough support muscles to get rid of whatever it was. In between comforting words and poorly hidden giggles, we were able to explain that this was the normal procedure for everybody, and that it was no wonder that he had been shocked to deliver his first shaped sample at the age of 12!

In that very moment we realized that he had been healed.

This could never have happened without a divine intervention. That he, who did not have any absorption of nutrients in his intestines, all of a sudden should have normal bowel function was unimaginable. After ten years of intravenous nutrition, his bowels should have shrunk and been completely out of order. We realized that Adrian had a new digestive system.

We were close to euphoric as we giggled our way into the kitchen where our other children were waiting for us, wondering how we could be so unsympathetic when facing desperate roars. We explained how Adrian was doing, and they stared at us in disbelief. Could this be possible? Was it really true that Adrian had been healed? They could hardly remember the time when Adrian was still eating. He could not tolerate food then either, but back then we did not know what made our youngest son sick. To his siblings, it was a distant memory they probably recalled mainly from the pictures in the family photo album. They were more used to the IV sets and pumps, of which they had specialized knowledge.

Thomas and I snuck off to discuss what had happened. We did not doubt for a second that Adrian had been touched by God, but how could we judge the extent of his healing? Was his digestion healed? His muscles? The epilepsy? The immune deficiency? The heart tachycardia? Was it everything, or was it just some?

How should we go about testing his healing? Should we take it carefully and give him a reduced amount of food for every meal? How big was this new stomach, anyway? Was it baby size or ordinary 12 year-old size? And what about his intestines? Would they require accustoming? Should we take any precautions? And how would suddenly eating again affect his immune system?

We had a thousand questions and no answers. We considered calling our excellent doctor, but concluded that we did not even know what to ask him.

Adrian came wandering out of the bathroom with a glorious

smirk on his face as the family jokes just exploded, stating that nobody could ever ask for a more solid evidence of a healing! Our many questions drowned in the cheering and the laughter as we prepared the breakfast. Suddenly Adrian was standing next to me with big, sparkling eyes that were fixed on what I held in my hand.

"What is that?" he twittered, "ham?"

His voice had a certain ring to it, and I could feel how he was beginning to comprehend that he had been healed.

"Yes," I answered. "Do you want some?"

He was delighted as he danced across the floor while carrying his plate. Never had honey-marinated, smoked ham ever been met with such enthusiasm. Heaven on earth had come to have a new meaning to Adrian.

The conference was coming to an end, but we had heard that Bethel's Healing Rooms would be open on the following day. We were told that it would be wise to get there early, as there was often a line to get in. When we got there at 8:10 a.m., we thought we were really early. It had taken a huge toll on us to get Adrian disconnected from the IV nutrition he was still getting, while preparing breakfast for the whole family, and then rushing everybody out on a Saturday morning, especially considering that we had not gone to bed until very late every night the entire week.

The Healing Rooms were open from 9 to 11 a.m., so we thought we had plenty of time as we got ready to park in front of the church. All of a sudden, we realized that there was a line of people all the way from inside the church and out in the parking area. Within seconds, the wheelchair, kids and sweaty adults were on their way to the line. We did not want to miss this.

We were handed sheets where we registered names and addresses, diagnosis if any, and symptoms. We filled out a form each. There were three small lines for diagnosis. Quick family council, we had to choose between Adrian's many diagnoses and decide which ones should be selected for the tiny lines. We never considered mentioning the digestive system as God had taken care of that already. We ended up writing down muscular atrophy, epilepsy and dyslexia. That last one was Adrian's suggestion—he decided to include it.

Each of us wrote on our lists what we needed prayer for.

Under the list of diagnoses and symptoms, there was a scale where you could state whether you were in pain at the moment and put down a number to describe the intensity of your pain.

As the line moved along, we were allowed into a reception room. There were artists painting in the middle of the room, and a small worship team was playing. One of the leaders of the Healing Rooms explained what would happen. Everything was said in a down-to-earth manner, while explaining what had previously happened in the Healing Rooms. We heard of miraculous healing, but the church never used it to promote itself. They were adamant that God should be given the glory for everything that had happened. Everybody was encouraged to contact their own doctor for examination to determine whether they were healed and to get medical documentation. If you were not healed, you were welcome back for more prayer. It felt good to be there.

Groups of 20-30 were taken into the next room where they received prayer. It was not a silent room. Some laughed, others cried. Several people tested if they had been healed by doing things that they had previously been unable to do. Some did pushups to see if arms and shoulders had been healed; others flexed their knees to check the function of their knees. Those who had been healed rejoiced, and all who were in the proximity rejoiced with them. If they were not healed, the prayer continued. We sat and watched everything that was going on. It was impossible not to smile in such a lovely atmosphere.

Finally, it was our turn. As we had several last names in our family, it got complicated as they searched for the individual lists of each family member. One man who sat with us commented that several of us were wearing glasses and said that we could start by praying that our eyesight would improve. All of a sudden, we were hit by our Norwegian-ness and commented that we had not put that on our list. He grinned and said that it was OK—we could still pray for it in addition to the other issues. In hindsight it sounds completely ridiculous, but it was as if we thought that we could not pray for that at the cost of anything else. But that is not how God is. A healing of sight does not come at the cost of a healing of muscular atrophy. But that was actually how we thought. It was as if we would not pray for healing for something minor, because we had to "save" it for the major issues. Completely stupid, we eventually got that God is big enough to cover it all.

Two of our children got their vision healed almost instantly, while other family members still needed glasses. It was a fun and faith-strengthening encouragement to us. It felt like playing our way to faith. We had the approach of a child as we drew near to the Father, and we felt ready to receive whatever he had for us.

We were still waiting for our lists to arrive. The man who was sitting with us suddenly looked puzzled. He frowned and thought for a few seconds before he commented, "I feel like God is telling me to ask you about something that is actually against the rules of the Healing Rooms." He paused to think before saying, "But I have to go ahead and ask, anyway. Adrian, God is asking you: 'Do you want a snack?'"

There was a complete silence before we broke down in laughter. He looked confused, so we rushed to give him an explanation. Nobody in that room knew that Adrian had not been unable to eat for more than a decade, nor did they know that he had been healed two days earlier. In the course of the last couple of days, we had tried to slow down Adrian's appetite, as he was ready to orally vacuum clean everything that was remotely similar to food. We had tried to explain that it would be wise for him to limit himself to meals, and that he should eat food that was healthy for his body. After a giant consumption of chocolate chip cookies the day before, I had momentarily banned cakes and sweets from his diet. "If God has given you a new digestive system, you don't have to ruin it in a fortnight," this well-meaning mom said, full of good intentions. And now God was offering him snacks? Even in the Healing Rooms, where you were not supposed to bring food?

One of the people from the prayer team disappeared before coming back with a napkin filled with snacks. There was a rice cake with honey, some blueberries, and a chocolate cake.

"What would you like, Adrian?" the man asked while holding the napkin in front of him.

Adrian glanced briefly at the napkin before his hand shot forward to grab the chocolate cake and put it in his mouth. With chocolate icing covering half his face and beaming eyes, he exclaimed, "God said it was OK, Mom!"

I laughed. God did not do things halfway—he saw to all of it. He offered Adrian all the good things that he had missed out on. We sensed that he was offering us what we had missed out on, too, and that was not chocolate cake.

The lists had arrived, and we were prayed for, one by one. Through the previous six months, the muscles on Adrian's right side had weakened considerably. This enabled us to easily check his right side against his left side to see if there were any changes to his muscles. We noticed a stronger grip and notably more stamina in his muscles, but we could not judge the extent of what had happened. The prayer team encouraged us to get Adrian's own medical team to examine him and determine whether he was healed.

Every member of our family was impacted by what we experienced in the Healing Rooms, and we all got to encounter God in a new way. It felt as if he had picked what we most wanted and giftwrapped it before waiting for us to open our present. It was as if he was standing there, leaning forward on his tiptoes and tripping as we tore off the paper. I am convinced that he laughed and clapped his hands when he saw our expressions as we opened our gifts.

We saw God in a new light. He was the living, tripping God who clapped his hands while showering us with his love. Daddy God came to meet us.

W e were supposed to stay in Redding for a week before leaving to explore the rest of California. As departure from Bethel drew closer, our kids began to grumble. They did not want to move on.

The church held three services every Sunday in summertime. Thomas and I agreed to go to two of them. The children protested— why could we not go to all three of them? They were used to going to services, but it had probably never even occurred to them that one might go to more than one service a Sunday. And now all of a sudden they wanted to go to *three*? They were hooked on the presence of God. They could not possibly imagine losing out on anything that God did.

We went to two services, and the presence of God lay like a cloud over the congregation. It cannot be described, but once you have experienced it, you recognize God immediately whether you knew him before or not. Once again our kids refused to go home after the service. We remained for hours, just because it felt good to be there. Eventually, we got them to tag along with us, and we went to our rented home to pack our things.

Packing went excruciatingly slowly. The children did not want to pack, nor did they want to leave. They did not get the point of leaving Redding. All the promises in the world of nice experiences and exciting surprises were not enough to motivate them to move on. Of course, they knew that God would go with us—it was not as if we were leaving him in Redding! But they also knew what they had experienced there, and they were unwilling to miss out on anything. Finally we reached an agreement. We would leave for four days before returning to Redding to go to the last services before going back to Norway. The kids were OK with that and more willing to cooperate.

Seeing how uncompromising our children were when it came to their search for God made us ponder. It was above everything. Once more, they led the way into a deeper fellowship with God. They showed a zealousness that served as an example for us to follow. We do not want to miss out on anything that God has for us. Not just for our own sake, but for the sake of others. We want more of God in order to bless others. That is when we fulfill our purpose.

D eparture was closing in. We started planning for our flight and packing all the equipment we needed to take, when it suddenly dawned on us that Adrian did not have to be hooked up to his IV line on the return flight. We could just pack everything in suitcases and send it as ordinary luggage. When I realized that, I felt weird. It was almost impossible to comprehend. We had lived with this for so long that we did not know any other way of living.

We had reduced Adrian's IV nutrition by 20 percent, but he continued to get connected every night. Now we decided to change the schedule for his IV nutrition in order for him to be able to make the long trip without having to be hooked up to his IV line. Usually the level of blood sugar dropped significantly after 12 hours without any IV nutrition, but this time we planned for him to eat during the flight. Because he would not be connected during the flight, we had no way of giving him IV analgesics in case he got sick. Nevertheless, we decided that this was the right thing to do. We felt calm as we discussed it.

Even so, as we entered the plane, we felt absolutely electric. We rejoiced as we could board without any tube sets, IV bags, pumps and bags. You know the expression that small children have on their faces as they are thrown up in the air, knowing full well that they will be landing safely in their father's arms? That's how we felt.

We had not traveled for long before the meal was served, and minutes afterward everybody could hear Adrian's loud comment to his sister: "You know how you always say that airplane meals taste like crap? I like it!" Our family laughed so hard, yet we were still relieved that most of the passengers did not understand any Norwegian.

One of our kids suddenly sat up straight in his seat. "He's done it! He promised he would make us whole again!" A pulsating, red heart arose from the shattered pieces of glass. The promise from the Christmas ornament had been fulfilled.

We began to get glimpses of the new future that awaited us, but we still did not know the extent of it. We could barely envision the outlines.

A NEW LIFE

July 2012

We argued about who would make the phone call to the doctor. Thomas lost. Usually, it was always nice to talk to our excellent doctor, but now we did not know what to say. In so many ways, it felt like maintaining steam within a boiling kettle. We had so much to tell that we practically boiled over, but instead we had to remain calm as we accounted for Adrian's medical status as well as for the events that had led up to these changes.

We knew that our doctor would be delighted to hear of Adrian's progress, but at the same time, he was responsible for the treatment that we were providing Adrian within our home. How would he relate to this?

I paced restlessly back and forth as Thomas made the call. He described what had happened and explained how Adrian now could eat ordinary food. He talked for a very long time and practically without any interruptions and it was clear that the other end of the line was unusually quiet. After a while, the doctor hesitatingly asked how much Adrian had eaten during the holiday. Thomas chickened out; I could see how his brain was working overtime as he mentally made a selection of all the things that Adrian had eaten while in the US. I noticed how he mentioned whole wheat bread, salads, and chicken, but that he failed to mention hamburgers, bacon, and chocolate chip cookies. He let the steam out gently.

Our doctor had followed Adrian ever since he was a baby. He knew perfectly well that even tiny amounts of food had been unimaginable for him. Adrian had been through a very thorough medical examination, and our doctor had done an excellent job of enabling us to take charge of the medical treatment. Now he also had to relate to his healing.

"We could go about this carefully. I don't suppose that would be incompatible with your experiences?" the doctor said.

Of course that was fine, and we appreciated that the doctor chose to monitor Adrian's health carefully now that he had begun eating. He scheduled an appointment for us the following week and told us what blood samples to order.

In the meantime, we had an appointment with Adrian's regular physiotherapist two days after our return from the States. She knew that we had been on holiday but knew nothing of what we had experienced during our stay. We asked Adrian not to tell her of any of it before she had examined him properly. He liked the idea.

The physiotherapist knew Adrian well. He had been seeing her for many years, and she had observed the continuous decay in his body with great concern. Through the last months she had stated that he was getting strain injuries. The muscles he had left still had to carry much more weight than they could take, and he had begun to ache in his hips and knees. Up until now Adrian had used his wheelchair mainly outdoors, and indoors if needed. The physiotherapist had several times pointed out to us that this was no longer enough. He would have to use the wheelchair indoors as well to relieve his joints.

"I feel a bit stronger in my arms and legs, and maybe in my back, too," Adrian said. "Could you check?"

Sure, the physiotherapist was not puzzled. She had tested him just before we left for our holiday and knew exactly how he had been before we left. She removed the heat packs and began testing his legs. First once. She waited a bit before testing him again. Thoughtful frown. Then she tried for the third time before exclaiming: "Where did all these strong, new muscles come from, Adrian?"

It was Adrian's turn to let out steam. He boiled over as he told her about everything we had experienced, that he could now eat without getting sick, and that he had much more strength than he used to have. Our precious physiotherapist rejoiced with him, and then she systematically tested him to check his muscles. She confirmed that he was much stronger than before and that there was new muscle tissue where there had been none.

Thomas and I had felt these muscles in his back already two days after he had received prayer, but we had not mentioned it to anyone else. When we stroked his back, we had noticed how the bone was more covered than it had previously been. However, we were not sure as to whether it was muscle tissue or fat that caused such a change. No matter—it would have been a miracle either way because Adrian had previously been diagnosed with not having any absorption of nutrients in his intestines. It felt like muscle tissue, but that was almost too good to be true. We had decided to keep it in our hearts and ponder it.

Now the physiotherapist confirmed it to be true. New muscle tissue had appeared. This does not happen in a child with a progressive disease. It was not difficult for our physiotherapist to see that something had happened that could not be logically explained.

She monitored Adrian closely in the time to come and made sure that Adrian got to exercise his muscles adequately as they developed. The day she decided to put Adrian on a regular workout schedule was a day of celebration for us.

When Adrian came walking into the doctor's office, the doctor went quiet. He observed Adrian as he sat down and then said thoughtfully, "You don't usually sit there."

"No," Adrian grinned, "I usually sit in that corner 'cause that's the only place where the wheelchair can fit!"

Eight years had passed since the last time Adrian had been able to walk on his own two feet into the doctor's office. The doctor got to hear the whole story of what had happened, and the changes it implied in Adrian's life. He examined him and made a plan for follow up.

"You understand that I have to relate to this as a medical doctor, Adrian?" he said.

That was easy to understand, and it enabled us parents to fully focus on all the wonderful changes that happened daily in our little boy. His digestive system had been healed instantly. What went on in the rest of his body was a process, but the muscle tissue augmented much more quickly than the levels of food intake and activity entailed. His body changed so fast that it was hard to keep track. Every time I embraced him I had to tell myself that this was my son. The boy who used to literally melt into my arms all of a sudden felt completely different. Now, whenever I held him in my arms, I could feel the muscles and strength in his body. It was no longer I who embraced him, we embraced each other.

We were invited to a summer camp one month after Adrian's healing, and we observed how he was getting stronger every day. We had been there before, and a lot of people recognized Adrian. This summer they found themselves intrigued by the fact that the wheelchair was often left empty in the yard while Adrian ran around somewhere playing with the other children. Once in a while, adults approached him and asked him to tell them what had happened. Adrian smiled and gently asked them to accompany him as he walked over the lawn. Then he stopped, and pointed in our direction, and said, "That's my Mom and Dad. You are welcome to ask them any questions, but I'm kind of busy playing,."

Then he ran off. Sometimes the adults came over, and we had some good conversations about everything that cannot be logically explained. Other times they snuck away, apparently somewhat annoyed. That was OK. We were happy to see that Adrian managed to decide for himself how available he wanted to be.

I was standing waiting for my family when a woman approached me. She was friendly but reserved.

"I would never have taken her to receive prayer," she said of her handicapped child. "That would be like saying that she's not good enough. I love her just the way she is."

And in that very moment, this distance appeared between us. A quantum leap between two mothers. On one hand, the woman who would never have done this to her child, who would never devalue her handicapped child by taking her to receive prayer. On the other hand, I, who had allowed my child to seek prayer when he wanted to, and who now rested my gaze on the boy who ran across the lawn.

There was an accusation floating in the air. Did I not love my child enough to let him remain sick? Was that to be considered the expression of the ultimate love?

A few months earlier, I too had worried about whether Adrian would feel devalued if we took him to be prayed for. At the same time, we wanted to support him if and whenever he was ready for it. She did not want to take her daughter to receive prayer, and I respected that. But it got me thinking. Was her child synonymous with her handicap? With her disease? We had made sure that Adrian was at peace with his illness, teaching him that he should never hide it or try to compensate for whatever he was unable to do. He was himself. But certainly he was more than his handicap.

It would have been easy to argue with her. To tell her that we by no means had dragged Adrian along to receive prayer. To elaborate on how we loved our wonderful little boy just as much whether he was sick or healthy. I could have elaborated on everything we had done to ensure that Adrian and his siblings were well cared for, that they got to live, flourish, and develop their individuality. I could have crushed her with the stories of pre-packed luggage ready for whenever we had to rush off to the nearest hospital; of air ambulances and helicopters; of the fear of missing a symptom or in some other way contributing to making this vulnerable life even more fragile; of analgesics with no effect; of roars of pain that stopped me from recognizing the sound of my own child; of the constant state of emergency. I could tell her about living like a fugitive of war, constantly listening for shootouts and new attacks.

I decided not to. She was a lioness, a mother who loved her child, a mother who had to fight with tooth and nail to make sure that her child was well. I recognized it and respected it. It had been my own situation for a long time.

I listened to her while she told me of her child. It was never hard to understand how proud she was of her daughter. That shone through. I was happy on behalf of the child, because she had a mother who always focused on her best. She ended with a shrug of her shoulders. Her comment was left floating in the air, almost like a dare.

I could have held Adrian in front of her, this happy, confident boy who had been through so much. I could have shown him off, almost like a trophy, saying: "We cannot have done *everything* wrong!" But it was not about us. It was not about Adrian either. It did not even have anything to do with what God had done.

Just as we had been unable to pray for Adrian's healing while taking care of all his medical needs, this mother could not bear to pray for the healing of her child. That was OK. The child was just as valuable anyway, and the mother's love could not have been greater. I did not know what God would have done. But I was starting to understand that his plans for us are way greater than we could ever imagine.

As I strolled away from the conversation with the lioness, I was reminded of another conversation that had taken place almost a month earlier. Even while in the U.S., I had started dreading that exact conversation.

In our hometown there were three children who were treated with intravenous nutrition. As far as we knew, none of us were related, and several of us parents were newcomers in town. Nevertheless, three boys in the same town had severe health issues that had to be treated with IV nutrition. Of these, Adrian was the only one who could not tolerate any food at all. The other two had some absorption of nutrients in their intestines.

We parents quickly found a "birds of a feather flock together" relationship. We spent time together discussing symptoms, development, research, and treatment options. The mothers in particular formed a close-knit friendship, and we talked several times a week—sometimes several times a day—not only about our children, but about everything. We shared the concerns for our children. We shared it all. They knew us inside and out, and nevertheless they chose to remain our friends. I truly loved these women.

I dreaded meeting them. How could I convey to them what had happened during our stay in the States? They knew how sick Adrian had been. They had processed with me whether he would be able to go through with such a journey. They had agreed to our conclusion that it would be important to make the trip that year because most likely he would be unable to go through with such a strenuous journey the following year. What would they say now? Would they believe what I had to say? How should I tell them what had happened?

The same day we landed in Norway, the text messages came ticking in with questions of how our holiday had been. I considered for a while before answering: "Back home again! ☺ We have had a great time! By the way, did I mention that Adrian has eaten three slices of bread today? Love, Marian."

It took an hour and a half before any of them answered. Then I got a text saying that they were happy that we had had such a nice trip, but that they did not know whether I was kidding or if Adrian had been healed. I sent a short text message: "I am not kidding."

The phone rang off the hook. We arranged to meet a few days after. I lay awake at night before I was due to meet the women. A thousand thoughts passed through my head. Would they be upset that Adrian had been healed while their children were still sick? It was impossible to fall asleep.

We met at a diner downtown, and they did not waste a second. The questions came tumbling at me from the very first second we met. It did not matter where we had been or what we had experienced. They wanted to know what had happened to Adrian. As I told the story, they kept asking questions. They wanted to know how we had proceeded to check if Adrian could tolerate food, what we had given him, how we had reduced the intravenous nutrition, how his body had developed, and what the blood samples looked like. I was examined for three hours. In spite of my nervousness, I had to smile. Adrian would never have to worry. If Thomas and I ever did anything wrong to him, these two women would crucify me. They were his guards. What a wonderful friendship!

I admitted that I had been dreading seeing them, and that I had been scared of inflicting more grief upon them as my child had been healed while theirs were still sick.

They looked at me as if I had lost my mind. They were thrilled to learn that Adrian was healthy, and both of them claimed to have some ownership in my son, implying that they, too, had experienced a healing!

That is when Adrian came walking into the diner with his dad and siblings. He was licking eagerly on an ice cream while his eyes were beaming. His wheelchair remained at home.

In that very same moment it dawned on his bonus moms that he had been healed. It was as if a window had been opened up wide and fresh air filled the room. In an instant these two moms had gotten new hope for their boys. As one of them said, "If this can happen to Adrian, it can happen to our son, too. I know you, and there's nothing special about you guys!"

I laughed! It was true. We were not special, and it had nothing to do with us. It was all about God and what he was doing. As we ran into people, we encountered all kinds of reactions as we told them about what had happened to Adrian. Some were thrilled. Others were shocked and quiet. Some, like the lioness, were dismissive and maybe a bit hurt. Nobody remained indifferent.

We were OK with that. We learned to recognize that people's different reactions had nothing to do with us, but with them, their lives and expectations, and their relationship with God. We understood that some needed more time, and that was all right. Others were tremendously happy and longingly ready to embrace the intervention of God in their own lives.

Some Christians inquired whether we feared that the healing would not last. We took it as an expression of concern, and while accepting the affection, we refused to embrace the statement. No, we were not afraid of that. We had seen how God took it all. We had been trained to observe, and we knew what we had seen. We had seen an Almighty God creating muscle tissue out of nothing and given new life to useless intestines. So many things in Adrian had been completely changed. We no longer feared the future—we looked forward to it!

Our family had reencountered God in a completely new way. One day, as we were discussing the experiences at Bethel, I asked Adrian, "If you had to choose between being healed and the presence of God, what would you choose?"

He did not even look up from his plate as he answered, "The presence of God. Without a doubt."

It was not a rehearsed answer, or something he thought that I expected him to say. It came from his heart. Thankfully, he did not have to choose.

T he next few weeks became slightly too challenging for us, as Adrian got the shingles. Adrian was outraged by the Norwegian common name for it, which was "Hellish fire," and was determined to call it by its Latin description, *herpes zoster*. He was not about to accept that dreadful name!

The tiny rash spread from his stomach towards the ribs, but it was never painful, and Adrian was in good shape. Due to his medical history, the doctors decided to treat him, and we started on IV medication before switching to pills.

As the shingles progressed, Adrian's liver values increased, which often happens as a result of infections. Our doctor was alarmed by this and feared that Adrian once again would get acutely ill because of his immune deficiency. Considering what had happened before, it was a natural line of thought, but we were in doubt as to what to expect. After all, Adrian was healed. Was he healed from it all, or just from some of his medical problems? We did not know, so we had to hope for the best but prepare for everything.

As the liver values continued to increase, the doctors discussed whether it was the food that made Adrian sick. He was still getting a reduced amount of intravenous nutrition every night according to the reduction plan made by his doctor. Now the hospital wondered if Adrian ought to go back to receiving all nutrition intravenously. As long as he had been living on IV nutrition, he had been healthy.

It was difficult for us as parents. We felt quite confident that it was the virus and the treatment causing the increasing liver values, and not the food. Nevertheless, we realized that no matter the cause, it could still trigger a serious autoimmune response from the diagnosed immune deficiency. We could not know if he still had it.

We were not going to gamble with Adrian's health in any way, but in this case, the map did not correspond with the terrain. The healthy boy we had in front of us bore little resemblance to the critically ill boy that had previously been bedridden with spiking liver values. He was running, climbing, and playing, and he was in great shape!

The results from the blood tests indicated differently, but we knew our son, and we felt confident that he would be fine. We decided to feed him ordinary food as we had been doing for the last weeks while at the same time continuing to reduce the intravenous nutrition. We took frequent blood tests and monitored his condition closely, but Adrian was doing really well. After a while, the liver values decreased and stabilized.

We learned something from that process. We have always been rational and responsible in our approach to Adrian's disease, as we were on this occasion. Still, we allowed ourselves to be guided by our gut instinct and our inner conviction to a larger extent than had been the case before, while still following up on the medical treatment prescribed by the hospital.

It was as if the worries just did not affect us. We felt that Adrian was doing well, and that left us at ease, even though the blood work indicated quite differently. In spite of all our experiences with him getting extremely ill very quickly, we no longer feared what could go wrong. It was more a question of what God was going to do next.

Our perspective had changed. The inner life became as

important or even more important than whatever happened in the outside world. What we sensed on the inside became normative. Our circumstances might be chaotic and unpredictable, but if we felt peaceful, we let ourselves be guided by that inner peace. Equally, if we felt that it was time for action even though there was no apparent need for it, we rolled up our sleeves and got going. We practiced letting ourselves be guided by the inner dialogue.

I mentioned this to a friend, and she studied me carefully.

"Hmm," she said slowly. "Do you often hear those voices in your head?"

That was hilarious and easy to laugh at, but nevertheless, it felt like throwing out an anchor. We became much less vulnerable to the waves. We certainly were surrounded by waves. Our life was about to be completely turned around! We had gone from having a very sick child to having a healthy and active son. From now on, life would be lived differently, and we had a lot to learn.

Fall 2012

We had built up our life to make sure that we would be able to care for our boy and be there for him. Thomas had been receiving financial aid for more than ten years to take care of Adrian, and both of us had been working at home to make it work. We had constructed a huge, wheelchair-adapted house with an elevator out of concern for Adrian and his progressive disease. Now the needs were completely changed.

Three days before Adrian was due to start at a new school, we met with the principal. She had accepted him as a student, knowing that the classroom and entrance would have to be remodeled and made accessible for a wheelchair. That was no easy task, as it was an old building. Even though the plan had originally been for a teacher from the school to teach Adrian in our home, we had arranged for him to be a part of his class whenever he was able to. The headmaster of the school was brilliant at seeing possibilities where others only saw obstacles. To her, the impossible would only take slightly more time. When we sat down to tell her what had happened during the summer, she dried her tears of joy and rejoiced with us. Together we decided that Adrian should start school with his class. Initially, he would be there for three hours a day. It did not take a week before he presented himself in the principal's office demanding to get more hours. He was thrilled and felt stronger than ever before. After a short period of time, he followed the complete schedule at school. He went from being taught by a teacher at home for six years to having full days at school with a wonderful bunch of 12-year-olds.

As delighted as we were with Adrian's fantastic development, it became apparent that our life was changing radically. We still did not know how. Nevertheless, we had to make adjustments, meeting with the social security services and with authorities from the local community to update them on our situation and inform them that we would no longer need all the assistance we were receiving. It felt like working our way through a mathematical equation with 23 unknown factors!

We had received a notice before all this happened. Two months prior to Adrian's healing, I felt God urging us to sort through our finances. At the time, I expected it to be God preparing us for something that he had in store for us, but I had no clue as to what it was. We carefully examined all aspects of our finances and calculated the income that we would need to have in order to handle our expenses. We agreed that we had quite a tight budget and that our huge mortgage did not allow us much leeway. So we parked the discussion. We decided that unless something radical happened, we would continue as we were. If anything changed, we would discuss it again because we knew that God had told us to be on the alert.

Then Adrian was healed, and we suddenly understood why we had needed the heads up. Right there in the middle of this very uncertain time of our life, we had to start making plans for the future, in spite of not knowing anything of what lay ahead of us. It felt good to be safely anchored.

We started the process of selling parts of the house. We no longer needed this house with the enormous wheelchair-adapted surfaces, and at the same time, that would enable us to reduce our huge mortgage. Thomas had to find a new job as soon as possible. It was surreal to him to look for a new job after having taken care of his son's medical needs for so many, many years. It is always demanding to start in a new job. It is even more demanding when you have been working at home for 10 years.

Concurrently, we had to terminate and disassemble the support schemes and equipment. We no longer needed the elevator that stretched all through our house. Or the ceiling lift from Adrian's bedroom to his bathroom. Or the electric wheelchairs. Or his motorized outdoors terrain wheelchair that he had used for trips in field and forest. Or countless other pieces of equipment that used to be essential to our daily life. We returned his handicap-adapted car because we no longer needed it. We purchased an ordinary used family car instead.

After a short while, we no longer needed the intravenous pumps. The intravenous nutrition was replaced by plain food in his stomach. Adrian's muscle tissue developed quickly—a lot faster than what nutritional intake and physical activity solely would accomplish. The chest muscles increased so rapidly that it caused the port chamber that was connected to his central line to be torn lose from its position, requiring it to be surgically removed.

Five minutes after Adrian woke up from anesthesia from this procedure, he surprisedly commented, "This feels completely different. This time I don't feel like I've run a marathon."

Usually he would have been exhausted and sick for several days afterward. This time, four hours after this surgery, we were sitting at home in our own living room. A couple of days later, he was climbing trees, something that he had never ever been able to do when he had the subcutaneous IV port. He ran along while holding a hand over his new incision so it would not rupture. His body was completely changed.

The day we could write Social Services and our local community and terminate all financial support schemes was a day of celebration! It felt wonderful to tell them what had happened to Adrian while explaining that we no longer qualified for any support measures. He was healthy!

We realized why God had given us the heads up, and we were very grateful for being somewhat prepared for the financial turnaround that lay ahead of us. We trusted that he would provide for us, while we administered well what he already had trusted us with.

So many things were waiting to be experienced for the very first time! I was waiting on our porch as Adrian came back from walking the dog on his own for the first time.

"Don't you trust me?" he wondered.

Of course I trusted him. I just enjoyed the view!

His big brother wanted to know if Adrian still had an immune deficiency.

"I don't know what I've been healed from," Adrian said with a puzzled look, "but I think I might have been healed from that, too. I can do all kinds of things now without getting sick."

"Great!" his brother beamed. "Then it's your turn to pick up the dog crap!"

There is nothing like family to keep you grounded.

There were so many firsts. First time on ice skates. First sleepover on his own. First communion. He had never before been able to eat the bread or drink the wine. First time to the movies without his parents in the immediate vicinity. First birthday celebration with his class. This time he could actually taste the cake. First time on his own alpine skis. It was time to get rid of the sit-ski that Dad and Adrian had been using for skiing downhill. From now on, he would stand on his own two feet. In the garage a bicycle was waiting for a sunny day. Last time he had done some bicycling on his own, he was three years old. At the time, he had the tiniest bike with support wheels on. He hardly got to use it before he became too weak to ride, and a wheelchair had replaced the bike. Now we prepared ourselves to run alongside the bicycle to teach our 12-year-old how to ride it.

It was a fabulous time! At the same time, we had to deal with all these issues! We talked about our "luxury issues"—these challenges that we now faced because Adrian had been healed. We balanced carefully between enjoying the moment and planning ahead.

Our son was healthy! He had received the gift of a future!

We had been given hope for the future. Only those who have lived without can possibly understand the implications of such a gift. We knew that the best was ahead of us.

S everal reporters approached us in the weeks after Adrian was healed. We held back because we wanted to make sure that he had enough time to get used to being healed and to develop at his own pace without any media attention.

But after a short period of time, we realized how many were actually talking about what had happened, and it became very important to us for the truth to be told. A lot of people wondered what had happened. Had we changed the treatment? Was that the reason for Adrian's healing?

One thing was certain: There was nothing that we or others had done that had led to this change. We, who would have done anything to get Adrian healthy, had been completely powerless when facing his disease. If there had been anything that we could have done to stop it, we would have a long time ago!

We had tried everything. Collaborating with doctors in various hospitals over the years, we had tested whether the bowel function had matured or changed. We had given him minuscule amounts of food to no avail. Adrian had never been scared of eating. He had always hoped that his situation would change. There was no sign of any eating disorder—it was the pain and the physical reactions that prevented him from absorbing nutrition the ordinary way.

He had received physical treatment for several years. After his first visit to the physical therapist, he needed intravenous painkillers all through the night. Even a light massage resulted in cramps and muscle aches the following day. The task of the therapist was limited to reducing muscular spasms, fibroids, or excessive inflammation.

Thomas had been taking Adrian to the hot water therapeutic swimming pool twice a week to stimulate and maintain muscles and joints. They played and exercised in the warm water, but as time went by, Adrian no longer had the strength to play. The exercise was turned into relaxation in the hot water pool. Even then Adrian had to sleep afterward from exhaustion. It was as if his muscles had been preprogrammed to decrease.

For the last few years, we had given him exactly the same nutrition, the same medication, the same treatment. Adrian's disease progressed regardless. No matter what we did, we were unable to make a difference.

If we had known how to cure his disease, did anyone really believe that we would not have? In that case, they did not know us.

Nothing we had done had healed Adrian. Nevertheless, he had been healed. What God had done was so amazing beyond words. We wanted him to receive the credit.

We accepted the invitation from two newspapers; a local newspaper called *Stavanger Aftenblad*, and a national newspaper called *Vårt Land*. The reporters contacted the doctors who had been heavily involved in Adrian's treatment at two different hospitals. Both confirmed the medical history and the radical improvement that had taken place, but none of them could provide a medical explanation for his healing. One of the doctors stated: "Regardless, I find it difficult to understand how his bowels normalized so quickly. An intestine that is not in use over time will normally stop working, just as muscles that are not being used will shrivel and disappear. Adrian started eating head-on by eating hamburgers."

The newspapers also interviewed the physiotherapist. She was outspoken: "This is a wonder from God. A miracle; nothing less."

THE
DIFFICULT
QUESTIONS

A ll the questions remain. Why did Adrian survive? Did God not warn us that he would die?

If he planned to heal him, why did he not do it earlier? Why would he let a little boy suffer like that? *"If God can, and he doesn't want to, what kind of God is he then?"* Could he not do it? Did he not want to? And then, who would he be?

What about Adrian's dream? Was that only a product of the vivid imagination of a child? Why, then, did the authority of what he said overwhelm us parents? Was it only a vain attempt to make sense out of the utter senselessness? We would have embraced the idea of any future other than losing Adrian. The thought of not holding him in our arms left us torn to bleeding pieces. Even though I found some comfort in the thought of him being with Jesus, the fear of the possible void in my arms and in my soul was sufficient to crush a mother's heart. I would never have accepted what he said had I not recognized it to be true. So why did it not happen?

My thoughts wandered off to Adrian's favorite story in the book of Kings. Did God not tell Hezekiah that he would die? Did he not change his mind when the king pleaded for his life? Did that imply that what the prophet had said at first was not true?

No, God always speaks the truth. He is incapable of anything else.

Our Father chooses to listen to us. Not because he has to, but because he wants to. He created us to be in fellowship with him.

Only when we remain in communion with him do we become whole. Just as we parents love to listen to the inner thoughts of our children, he listens to us.

I share Adrian's fascination with King David. I am so smitten by the way he knew God. It is as if he lived in a symbiosis with the Creator. David expresses God's heart in the book of Psalms in a way that we can relate to. It is as if he expresses God's longings with his own words, maybe because he longed for the same. Those we spend time with impact us.

Was it David's idea to build a new temple, or was it God's will? Or did God lay down a longing for a new temple in David's heart, causing him to pray according to God's will? The result was, nevertheless, that God answered David's prayer, and he blessed his plans. He observed with joy how David prostrated himself before him and praised him, even though God had said that this would be the task of the priests only. David was created in God's image, as are we. When we live in the presence of God, our dreams will be a response to the longing that the Father carries for us. He listens and acts.

Does God allow himself to be moved by our prayers? Absolutely. He hears every sigh and every longing. He is our Daddy!

Why did he not heal Adrian before? I cannot answer that. I simply do not know. That is one of the questions that I have reserved for Papa God when he takes me home.

He did not have to heal Adrian. We loved our little boy just as he was; to us he was perfect. He perceived his life to be good in spite of his disease and did not miss what he had never experienced. God did not have to heal him to convince us; we already loved our Papa God. Neither sickness nor pain could ever change that.

So was that why he healed him? Because God knew that

we already loved him? Of course not. Nothing we accomplish will ever make us worthy of God's love. Our love for him is only a pale reflection of his love for us. We love because he loved us first. Even before we knew him, he loved us and watched over us.

It is easy to spot God when life is easy. When you are free of pain and surfing the ups. God is so clearly recognizable in the sunny seasons; gratitude comes so easily.

But where is he when life is tough? Or worse: When the nights become painfully sleepless and you can no longer find hope or meaning? What about when life feels infinitely difficult, maybe even unbearable? Did he sign off? Put life on hold while he is busy doing something else?

It is our testimony that God has been close even in the dark season. King David wrote: "He made darkness his covering, his canopy around him – the dark rain clouds of the sky." (Psalm 18:11) He gave us hidden treasures and riches stored in secret places, just as he had promised. He did not come with shouts or vivid colors. He just was. In the silence and the pain, he was there. He met us at the deep end.

When Adrian was healed, it was time for an outrageous dance of joy! But even back when he was sick, we danced with the Father. It was a quiet, close dance where I could lean my head toward him as my tears wet his chest. Tears for my healing, but without power to heal my boy. All these tears that the Father has put into a bottle. It was an intimate dance where he was mine and I was his. I was wrapped in his loving embrace.

I n the locker room after the first PE class, one of the boys kept staring at the many scars covering Adrian's torso.

"You sure must have fallen off your bike a lot of times," he exclaimed.

Adrian grinned as he explained that those were scars after surgery. He had about 40 of them covering his chest and stomach. In addition to that, he had a huge scar on his thigh after a muscle biopsy.

Adrian used to refer to them as his wounds of war. We had taught him to be proud of his scars. They gave evidence of what he had been through.

Ever since he was little, we had been determined to give him an identity that would include his disease. We did not want him to feel that he had to hide his illness or to exhaust himself trying to manage whatever he would be unable to do. Adrian had developed a relaxed attitude toward the disease and his own body. He was self-confident.

Now we would have to teach him how to live with his healing. It may sound easy, and in many ways it was. However, it would require a consciousness to the fact that Adrian was a child who had his life turned upside-down. Even good things require learning how to live with them.

It was a shock to Adrian when he realized how many people knew of what had happened to him. Regardless of us, the news of his healing spread like a wildfire. It took us all by surprise, but at the same time, we recognized the consequences. People got hope, not from us, but from God.

We had always lived our lives openly and transparently, and many had followed the progression of Adrian's disease. The many people that knew him felt that they took part in all the good that happened to him. Many had been praying for Adrian for years, and we had sensed how that had kept him alive.

We were especially grateful that all of Adrian's grandparents got to experience that he was healed. It moves me to think of these good people who daily had placed their grandchild in front of God, year after year, reminding him of his promises and praying once again for a touch, a caress, a wonder, a life. They were heard.

Adrian's healing is not only about boundless prayers in Bethel Church. It is also about grandparents sitting at the kitchen table with their hands folded in prayer. It is about children including Adrian in their prayers before going to sleep at night. Of siblings who intuitively chose prayer as their first and best option. Of people who loved us, but who loved the Father the most.

It is about despair that is being yelled across the fjords, and of sighs that drift off with the wind. Of tears in a bottle. Of him who will not break a bruised reed and not snuff out a smoldering wick.

It is not even about Adrian. This story is about him who takes what is broken and makes it whole.

> *May these words of my mouth and the meditation of*
> *my heart*
> *be pleasing in your sight,*
> *Lord, my rock and my Redeemer.*

> *–Psalm 19:15*

APPENDIX

Stavanger, 26.04.2016

31.03.16 Brev om pasient v/dr. Øymar / wks

To whom it may concern

This is a short review of the medical history of Adrian ███████, born ██05.2000.

He has a long and complicated history which difficult to reveal in all details, this summary is an overview and a confirmation of the principal medical history. The parents will have the full details.

The history kan be devided in symptoms from different organs, but we consider that this has had a common basic cause which has not fully been revealed.

1. Gastrointestinal.
From birth to about 6 months og age he was fully breastfed and with a normal development. When introducing solid foods he showed severe gastrointestinal reactions and after a period with nutritian via tube he has been on a full total parenteral nutrition (TPN) from early life. This has been ongoing until 2012. During all these years he showed severe reactions to minor introduction of solid food of any kind, with diarrhoea, pain etc. He also seemed to react (hepatic) to the TPN, after adjustment to fishoil based TPN this was improved. He has also been in need of iron infusions.
The thorough investigation showed reduced gastrointestinal motility, but biopsies etc. did not reveal any basic explanation for the severe malabsorption and intoleranse.

2. Immunology.
From early life he had episodes of severe infections with high levels of C-.reactive protein, and blood culture positive bloodstream infections, probably related to catheter infections. During early life several treatments with intravenous antibiotics. During recent years before 2012 he had chronic neutropenia, treated wit leukocyte stimulating factor with effedt. During a period also infusion of intravenous gamaglobulin. During this period fewere infections. Except for the

Postadresse
Postboks 8100
4068 Stavanger

Webadresse:
www.helse-stavanger.no

Kontaktinformasjon
Barne- og
Ungdomsklinikken
Tlf: 05151

partial neutropenia, no specific immunologic condition was revealed.

3. Hemophagocytosis.

He had several episodes of severe hemophagocytosis (HLH), proved by pancytopenia, high levels of triglycerides and extremely high ferritin. Episodes were possibly trigged by infections, but also suspected to be triggered by the fat content of the TPN. After changing to fish based TPN he had fewer episodes. The episodes were considired as secondary HLH.

4. Neurological

He has been neurological disabled, during several years in need of a wheelchair except for minor fysical activity. Both motorical and intellectual exhaustion was profound. No specific or basic cause for this was shown, but was suspected to be a part of a basic mechanism related to energy metabolism. He also had attacks which was possibly related to epileptic seizure, but also hearth rhythm was investigated in relation to these attacks.

4. Basic cause.

As discussed above, we consider all his symptoms as a result of some basic deficit, it was suspected to be a mitochondrial disease but no specific cause was ever found. He had a thorough examination in several centres, including a full genetic work up.

5. Development since 2012.

During 2012 the family went to USA, during that stay he started eating and gradually during 1-2 subsequent months the overall oral intake was increased and the TPN reduced. He tolerated this well, blood test were normalised and stayed normal. Finally, he was on a normal oral intake and the TPN was stopped, and during the following time his blood test has been fine except for s slight microcytosis, though the hemoglobin is normal.
In parallell, his motor activity has increased and normalised. His muscle mass has normalised from hypotoni and atrophy to normal size and function. His growth has been normal.

Regards

Knut Øymar
Senior consultant in pediatrics /professor in pediatrics
Barne- og ungdomsklinikken
Helse Stavanger HF

Mottakere:

Godkjent av: overlege Knut Asbjørn Alexander Øymar

Postadresse
Postboks 8100
4068 Stavanger

Webadresse:
www.helse-stavanger.no

Kontaktinformasjon
Barne- og
Ungdomsklinikken
Tlf: 05151

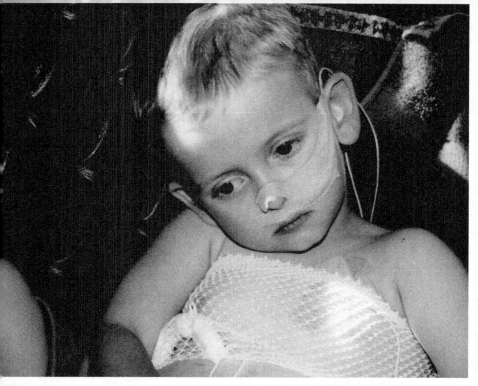

GOD
NÅ
SÅ
FOR
I DA
MED

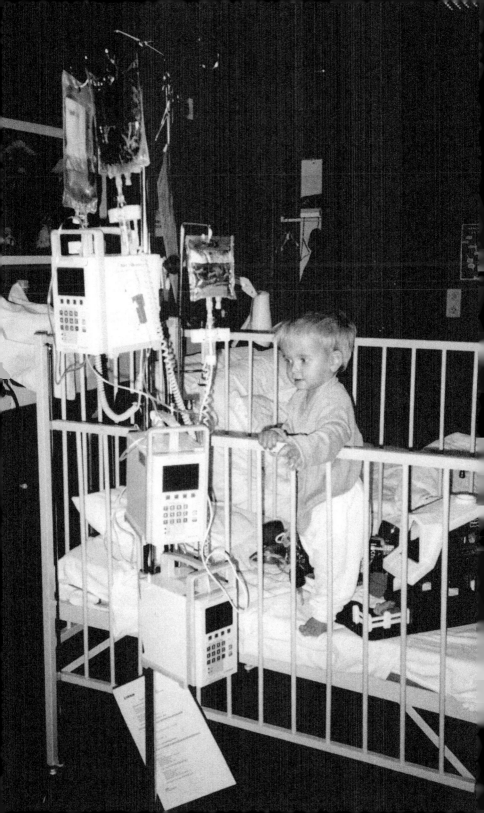

CPSIA information can be obtained at www.ICGtesting.com
Printed in the USA
BVOW06s1852101016

464659BV00012B/158/P